W9-CQH-947

Tomatoes

Elaine Elliot & Virginia Lee

Formac Publishing Company Limited
Halifax

In continuing the theme of the Flavours series of cookbooks, we have invited chefs from across Canada to share their recipes, and we thank them for their generosity. Each recipe has been tested and adjusted for the home cook.   — Elaine Elliot and Virginia Lee

Special thanks to **Craig Flinn**, chef and proprietor of Chives Canadian Bistro in Halifax, for preparing and styling the recipes photographed for this book.

Participating restaurants

British Columbia
Bishop's Restaurant, Vancouver, BC
Edgewater Lodge, Whistler, BC
The Mahle House Restaurant, Nanaimo, BC
Vij's, Vancouver, BC

Alberta
Suede Lounge, Edmonton, AB

Ontario
The Baldwin's Resort, Windemere, ON
Chez Piggy, Kingston, ON
The Epicurean Restaurant & Bistro, Niagara-on-the-Lake, ON
Hemispheres Restaurant and Bistro, The Metropolitan
   Hotel, Toronto, ON
Keefer Mansion Inn, Thorold, ON
Lakewinds Country Manor, Niagara-on-the-Lake, ON
Monet's Table, Sarnia, ON
Stone Road Grille, Niagara-on-the-Lake, ON

Quebec
Le Château Bonne Entente, Ste. Foy, QC

New Brunswick
Inn on the Cove & Spa, Saint John, NB

Prince Edward Island
Dayboat, Oyster Bed Bridge, PE
The Dunes Café, Brackley Beach, PE
Stanhope Beach Resort, Stanhope, PE
Flex Mussels, Charlottetown, PE

Nova Scotia
Acton's Grill and Café, Wolfville, NS
The Blomidon Inn, Wolfville, NS
Castle Rock Country Inn, Ingonish Ferry, NS
Chanterelle Country Inn, North River, St. Anne's Bay, NS
Chives Canadian Bistro, Halifax, NS
The Garrison House Inn, Annapolis Royal, NS
Inn on the Lake, Waverley, NS
The Italian Gourmet, Halifax, NS
Keltic Lodge, Ingonish Beach, NS
La Perla, Dartmouth, NS
MacKinnon-Cann Inn, Yarmouth, NS
The Old Orchard Inn Resort and Spa, Greenwich, NS
Opa Taverna, Halifax, NS
Rhubarb Grill & Café, Indian Harbour, NS
Tempest, Wolfville, NS

For Library and Archives Canada Cataloguing in Publication information, see p. 96

Formac Publishing Company Limited recognizes the support of the Province of Nova Scotia through the Department of Tourism, Culture and Heritage. We acknowledge the financial support of the Government of Canada through the Book Publishing Industry Development Program (BPIDP) for our publishing activities.

Formac Publishing Company Limited
5502 Atlantic Street
Halifax, Nova Scotia B3H 1G4
www.formac.ca

Printed and bound in Canada

Contents

Introduction

A Short History of the Tomato

How did the love affair between chefs and this fruit begin?

Like corn, squash and tobacco, the tomato plant is a product of the New World. Tomatoes are members of the Solanaceae family, which also includes eggplant, peppers, potatoes and tobacco. Our lush tomato, genus *Lycopersicon*, was originally a wild plant, native to the western slopes of the Andes, from Ecuador to Chile. The domesticated tomato plant as we know it was first developed by the Mexicans and Aztecs of Central America; when the Spanish Conquistadors arrived during the late fifteenth and early sixteenth centuries, they found the fruit already under cultivation.

These same Spanish explorers carried the seeds across the Atlantic Ocean to Spain, where the tomato was called "pomme dei Moro" or "Moors apple." Tomatoes were introduced to Italy where they were called "pomi d'oro" or "golden apples." This historic name leads scholars to believe that the early European tomatoes were, in fact, yellow in colour. Yet, so ingrained is this wonderful fruit in traditional Italian cuisine, one could almost believe it originated in an Italian garden. Today the "Mediterranean diet" is a cuisine that features tomatoes, both fresh and cooked in sauces.

Tomatoes became popular in southern Europe and the Mediterranean region during the early seventeenth century, but it would take many years for northern Europeans to appreciate their qualities. They dubbed the tomato the "stinking golden apple" or "wolf peach" and thought it poisonous. This idea probably came about because the tomato is a member of the nightshade family, whose plants contain toxic alkaloids. In truth, tomato foliage does contain the toxic glycoalkaloid tomatine, which is converted by enzymes to a nontoxic form in the fruit as it ripens. According to one seventeenth-century culinary book, eating a cooked tomato was safe but not recommended, while consuming a raw tomato would result in instant death.

It was inevitable that tomato seeds would make their way back across the Atlantic to the New World with European settlers, even though the fruit's reputation was suspect. It wasn't until the early 1800s that North Americans began growing and consuming the tomato in earnest, purportedly after a certain Colonel Johnson in Salem, New Jersey — in a demonstration of confidence — ate a basketful of tomatoes in full public view. The courageous man not only lived, he did not even suffer indigestion.

Fruit or Vegetable?

What is a tomato anyway? Is it a fruit or a vegetable? Botanically fruits are defined as the edible, seed-containing part of a plant, while vegetables are defined as the edible leaves, stems or roots of a plant. In the scientific world the tomato is a fruit, yet most people think of it as a vegetable. Tomatoes are not typically sweet like fruit and they are usually used in main course dishes, salads and soups or as an accompaniment to meat and seafood. We tend to think that if it looks like a vegetable and acts like a vegetable then it must be a vegetable.

And what about colour? When we think of tomatoes we think of 'red,' but a tomato can be yellow, pink, red or purple. It can be uniform in colour or it can be striped. Some tomatoes are small, others are large and meaty. Tomatoes suitable for making paste are elongated, others are fat and round.

Growing Your Own Tomatoes

Tomatoes top the list of fruits and vegetables cultivated in Canada's family gardens. Easy to grow, they can be found in community co-operative gardens, backyard plots, even in tubs and planters on doorsteps and high-rise balconies. Everyone loves a vine-ripened tomato, however small the garden. We encourage you to consider introducing Canadian seeds to your garden. Seeds of Diversity, a Canadian Heritage Seed Program has a long list of genuine Canadian-bred seeds and its website www.seeds.ca is filled with information on the topic.

More than 100 different heritage tomatoes are classified as Canadian, many introduced by Agriculture Canada between 1890 and 1980. These plants were either bred in Canada or have been grown long enough to adapt to our growing conditions. Provincial Departments of Agriculture offer advice on which varieties are most suitable for growing in a specific area.

Seed catalogues will also outline the many varieties suitable for planting in your area

What types of tomatoes should you add to your garden plot? Your choice is governed only by the space that you have available, but consider the old English rhyme…

'One to rot and one to grow
One for the pigeon, one for the crow'

Let this provide an inkling of how many plants to purchase. If you have a sunny patio or balcony you can satisfy your tomato-growing desires with species suitable for tub or pot growing. If you have a small garden plot you can allocate space for full-sized tomato plants, but be sure to take into account the size the plant will reach at maturity. Since most tomatoes are self-pollinating — that is, they are pollinated by insects such as bees, the wind or other natural mechanisms — it is not necessary to have more than one plant.

Most home gardeners take the easy route by purchasing transplants at garden centres. Transplants are seeds that have been planted in a greenhouse environment and grown to the stage where they can be moved to the garden when all danger of frost is past — mid-spring for British Columbia and Ontario's Niagara area; late May and early June for most Maritime and prairie gardens. Most varieties will produce fruit 60 to 70 days after transplanting, and more northern gardeners should choose plants that will ripen before autumn frosts.

The tags on the plants will provide all the information you need: how long to maturity, how much space each plant requires and so on. For example, a small plant like Tiny Tim needs only 18 inches (46 cm) between plants while larger plants such as Red Brandywine need a 5-foot square (1.5 m sq) area.

Choose plants that are deep green in colour and filled out, not long and spindly. It is wise to buy your transplants a week or so before you plan to plant them. This allows time to place them outdoors during the day, and move them indoors at night. This practice is called "hardening off," and it allows the plants to adapt to outdoor conditions gradually.

If possible, choose a cloudy day to transplant your tender plants. Tomatoes love rich soil so work in a generous amount of well-rotted manure or compost into the bed before planting. An application of lime is thought to help prevent the pesky Blossom end rot, a common condition that leaves an unattractive black blotch on the bottom of the fruit. Follow suggestions from your garden centre, till the soil and plant your transplants. Remember, tomatoes require full sun, and if at all possible do not plant them where either tomatoes or potatoes were grown in the past year. Gently set them deep into the soil and water well.

If planting varieties that require staking, known as "indeterminates," install your stakes or cages soon after setting them out so that the new roots are not damaged. Once indeterminate tomatoes begin producing they will continue to bear fruit throughout the summer and until the first hard frost. They benefit from gentle pruning to a single stem by breaking off side shoots as soon as they appear. You will notice these suckers growing between the main stem and leaf stem.

Non-staking "determinate" or bush varieties will grow to a certain height, flower, bear fruit and then stop. They do not require pruning and are suitable for pot growing. Whichever type you plant, weed regularly; some gardeners add mulch around the plants to keep weeds at bay and to hold moisture. Tomatoes require 1 inch (5 cm) of water per week and if Mother Nature isn't co-operative, water the plants weekly in the morning or early afternoon, allowing time to dry before dusk. Sit back and in about 60 days you will enjoy your first ripe tomato!

Popular Varieties for Home-Growing

Beefsteak:

A very popular indeterminate variety producing heavy yields of large solid fruit in a rich red colour.

Canabec or Canbec Rose:

A tomato that can stand cool nights in spring with a pink or rose colour. A popular Quebec choice.

Golden Queen:

A low-acid indeterminate tomato that starts to produce yellow tomatoes by mid-season. The fruit is nicely shaped, thick walled and meaty, with a very mild but pleasing taste.

Pilgrim:

Especially suited to northern climates this plant produces large, flavourful, smooth fruit.

Roma or Plum:

A bright red elongated fruit, meaty with few seeds, suitable for sauces and tomato paste.

Scotia

Introduced in the 1950s, Scotia is the most popular tomato grown in the Maritimes. The plant produces medium-sized bright red fruit with a high yield.

Sweet Baby Girl:

A determinate variety producing dark red fruit in long clusters over a 3 to 4 week period. Some feel these are the sweetest cherry-type tomatoes.

Sweet Million:

Early maturing with generous clusters of small, extremely sweet, deep-red fruit. This is a tall indeterminate plant and requires support.

Nutritional and Health Value

Tomatoes are an excellent source of vitamins and minerals: Vitamin A, which aids in bone and tooth development, contributes to healthy skin and aids night-vision; Vitamin B1, which releases energy from carbohydrates and aids growth; Vitamin B6, which helps with tissue formation and energy metabolism; and Vitamin C, which contributes to healthy bones, teeth and gums. Tomatoes are also a good source of Thiamine, Folacin, Potassium and Magnesium.

The substances that give tomatoes their bright colour — beta-carotene and lycopene — are being researched for their positive general affect on human health and contribution to reducing the risk of cancer. Research shows that lycopene helps suppress the oxidative radicals that play a role in degenerative diseases and aging.

A one-cup (250 mL) serving of tomato contains only 35 calories, 1 gram of cholesterol, 1 gram of fat, 2 grams of protein and 15 milligrams of sodium. One medium-sized fresh tomato provides 47% of the recommended daily allowance (RDA) of Vitamin C, and 22% of the RDA of Vitamin A.

Buying Tomatoes

What should you consider when buying a fresh tomato? Look for fruit that has bright colour, heavy weight for its size, plumpness and an aromatic fragrance. Choose firm tomatoes that are free of bruising and cracks. Store at room temperature, stem side up and use within a few days. Never store tomatoes in the refrigerator — it decreases flavour and makes for pulpy flesh. Before consuming, wash tomatoes with a minimal amount of water.

While most of the recipes in this collection feature fresh, vine-ripened tomatoes, tomatoes that have been stewed, canned and processed into sauces are an equally beneficial food source. They are an ideal substitute when fresh tomatoes are unavailable. Oil packed sun-dried tomatoes produce a powerful punch of flavour and are a suitable alternative for some recipes.

The Recipes

Between the covers of *Tomatoes* you will learn how to prepare and create a myriad of delightful and nutritious dishes using tomatoes and their products from farms across the nation. Heirloom Tomato and Sweet Onion Salad with Balsamic Syrup and Basil Oil from Vancouver's Bishop's Restaurant is superlative both in its flavour and its simplicity. Fresh tomato soups are offered in hot and cold form: when summer temperatures rise try Tempest World Cuisine's Yellow Tomato Gazpacho with Avocado Gelato; when cooler weather approaches prepare Creamy Tomato Soup from The Epicurean Restaurant & Bistro, Niagara-on-the-Lake.

A variety of flavourful luncheon and main-course recipes ensures the home chef a dish for every occasion. Levels of difficulty range from easy to complex. Seafood lovers will rave over the mussel recipes from Flex Mussels in Charlottetown: fresh local tomatoes and farm-raised mussels in their lemon-flavoured Medusa Mussels or brandy and cream-flavoured Bisque Mussels will leave you more than satisfied. Other lunch and dinner entrées feature tomatoes and their products with lamb, chicken and seafood.

This book will give the home chef an appreciation for the tomato in all its forms: fresh, dried, canned, in sauces or as a base for condiments. We offer thanks to the professional chefs who incorporate the tomato into their creative dishes and then share their recipes with us.

Fresh Tomato and Cilantro Soup, p.16

Soups and Salads

We continue to be delighted with the variety of recipes shared by chefs across Canada. Each growing zone features its own regional tomato varieties, but we are sure you will find fresh plump tomatoes from your area to do justice to these recipes.

In this section we invite you to be creative. Try one of the new coloured tomatoes featured in Yellow Tomato Gazpacho with Avocado Gelato from Wolfville's Tempest Restaurant. Or reunite your taste buds with tomato flavours of the past by preparing Heirloom Tomato and Sweet Onion Salad with Balsamic Syrup and Basil Oil from Bishop's Restaurant, Vancouver. So simple, but oh-so tasty.

Yellow Tomato Gazpacho
with Avocado Gelato

Tempest Restaurant, Wolfville, NS

Chef Michael Howell creates a very pretty yellow chilled soup in his adaptation of a typical Spanish gazpacho. It is essential to use fresh vine-ripened tomatoes for optimum flavour and consistency.

If yellow tomatoes are not available use red but substitute a roasted red pepper for the yellow pepper.

1 yellow pepper
2 ½ lb (1.25 kg) yellow tomatoes, chopped
¾ cup (175 mL) diced sweet onion (Vidalia, Walla Walla, Mayan etc.)
¼ English cucumber, peeled, seeded and chopped
2 stalks celery, strings removed and chopped
1 clove garlic, minced
2 tbsp (30 mL) sherry vinegar
2 tbsp (30 mL) sherry
½ tsp (2 mL) salt
¼ tsp (1 mL) white pepper
2 tbsp (30 mL) extra virgin olive oil
½ cup (125 mL) water
Avocado Gelato (recipe follows)

Preheat oven to 400°F (200°C). On a baking sheet, roast yellow pepper whole, turning 2 to 3 times until skin is charred, about 20 minutes. Remove from oven and place pepper in a plastic or paper bag, seal bag and set aside until cool enough to handle. Slide charred skin from pepper; core and remove seeds and membrane. Chop.

In a blender, combine all ingredients except Avocado Gelato and purée until smooth. (It may be necessary to purée in batches.) Strain purée through a sieve into a large bowl; cover and refrigerate up to 8 hours to allow flavours to blend. Adjust seasoning before serving.

To serve: portion gazpacho in soup bowls. Spoon a dollop of Avocado Gelato in the centre.

Serves 4 to 6.

Avocado Gelato

¾ cup (175 mL) simple syrup*

2 ripe avocados, peeled and pitted

2 tbsp (30 mL) diced red onion

2 tbsp (30 mL) minced cilantro

½ jalapeño pepper, seeded and diced

1 small tomato, peeled, seeded and chopped

½ tsp (2 mL) minced garlic

1 tsp (5 mL) minced shallot

2 tbsp (30 mL) chopped green onion

2 tbsp (30 mL) fresh lime juice

½ tsp (2 mL) salt

2 to 3 dashes Tabasco sauce

1 cup (250 mL) cold water

Prepare simple syrup in advance.

In a blender, combine all ingredients except simple syrup and purée until very smooth. Add simple syrup and combine. Chill 1 hour in refrigerator and then freeze in an ice-cream machine according to manufacturer's directions.

*To make simple syrup, in a saucepan combine ¾ cup (175 mL) water with ½ cup (125 mL) granulated sugar. Heat mixture, stirring constantly until sugar has dissolved. Cool.

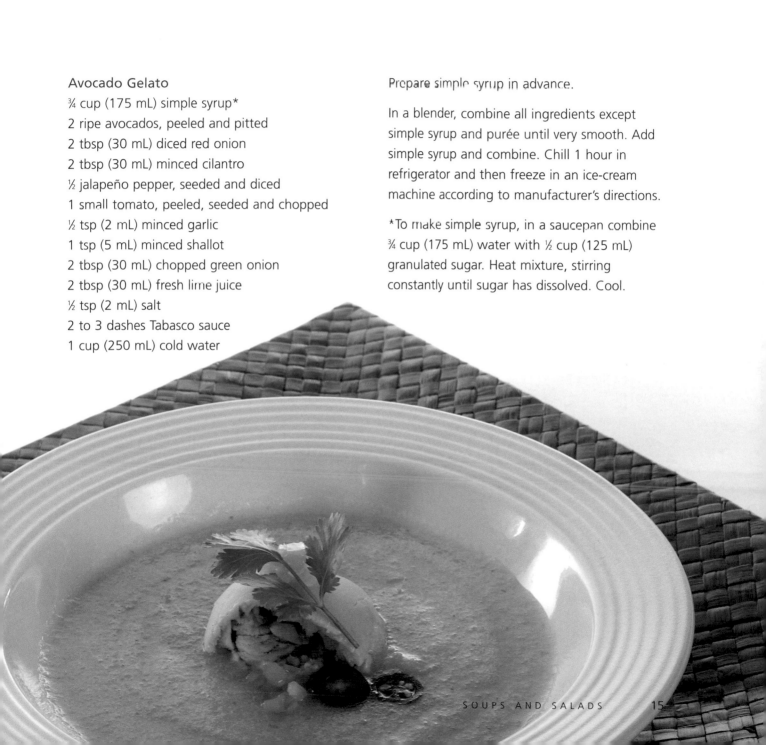

Fresh Tomato
and Cilantro Soup

The Dunes Café, Brackley Beach, PE

Chef Emily Wells comments: "This soup deserves garden-fresh tomatoes to be its best!" So wait you must for those delicious red beauties fresh off the vine. You will not be disappointed.

1 ½ lb (750 g) very ripe tomatoes
salt
2 tbsp (30 mL) extra virgin olive oil
1 ½ cups (375 mL) finely diced onion
2 cloves garlic, minced
3 tbsp (45 mL) all-purpose flour
4 cups (1 L) vegetable stock
1 cup (250 mL) loosely packed chopped cilantro
2 to 3 tbsp (30 to 45 mL) tamari, to taste (optional soy sauce)
1 tsp (5 mL) grated ginger root

Cut tomatoes in half horizontally, salt well and place cut side down on a cutting board 20 minutes. Squeeze seeds from tomatoes and discard; quickly rinse tomatoes with cold water to remove excess salt. Cut tomatoes into medium dice.

Heat oil in a saucepan over medium-low heat and sauté onion and garlic, stirring frequently, until lightly browned, about 6 to 8 minutes. Raise the heat to medium, add flour and stir until it has a nutty aroma, about 2 minutes. Whisk in stock, add tomatoes and bring to a boil. Add ½ cup (125 mL) cilantro; reduce heat to simmer, cover lightly and cook 30 minutes.

In a blender, purée soup in batches until smooth and creamy. If desired, strain through a fine-mesh sieve. Return soup to saucepan and bring back to serving temperature, stir in tamari and ginger and cook 1 minute longer. Cool to room temperature and refrigerate. If necessary, skim fat residue from surface.

To serve: ladle cold soup into chilled soup dishes.

Serves 6.

Sun-Dried Tomato & Fennel
Bisque

Acton's Grill & Café, Wolfville, NS

There are always alternatives when fresh-off-the-vine tomatoes are not in season. In this recipe Chef Drew Rudderham uses sun-dried tomatoes and tomato paste in combination with fennel and curry seasoning to create a warming soup for chilly fall and winter days.

1 fennel bulb, chopped
1 onion, chopped
2 celery stalks, chopped
2 carrots, chopped
½ cup (125 mL) oil-packed sun-dried tomatoes,
    drained and chopped
1 tsp (5 mL) curry powder
¼ tsp (1 mL) cayenne pepper
6 cups (1.5 L) beef-stock
3 tbsp (45 mL) butter
3 tbsp (45 mL) all-purpose flour
6 oz (180 mL) tomato paste
1 ½ cups (375 mL) heavy cream (35% m.f.)
½ tsp (2 mL) granulated sugar
salt and pepper
sour cream or crème fraîche, for garnish
fennel fronds, for garnish

In a large saucepan, combine first 8 ingredients, bring to a boil, reduce heat and simmer until vegetables are soft. Strain mixture. Remove vegetables to a food processor and return liquid to saucepan over low heat. Process vegetables, adding a small amount of liquid if necessary to obtain a smooth consistency; reserve purée.

Melt butter in a small saucepan, add flour, whisk and cook over low heat 2 to 3 minutes. Whisk tomato paste and 1 cup (250 mL) of hot vegetable liquid into flour mixture; return to vegetable liquid, whisking well to incorporate. Add heavy cream and reserved vegetable purée to soup. Bring to serving temperature and adjust seasoning with salt and pepper, and additional curry powder and cayenne if desired.

To serve: ladle into warmed soup bowls and spoon a dollop of sour cream or crème fraîche in centre of soup. Garnish with a small fennel frond.

Serves 6 to 8.

Creamy Tomato Basil Soup
with Cracked Peppercorns

Castle Rock Country Inn, Ingonish Ferry, NS

Prepare this soup when your garden is overflowing with vine-ripened tomatoes. Out of season, this "comfort food" may be prepared with canned tomatoes, which are usually on hand in any well-stocked cupboard. Who could ask for more on a blustery winter day?

7 cups (1.75 L) peeled and diced tomatoes
 (optional diced tinned tomatoes with juice)
2 tsp (10 mL) baking soda
⅓ cup (75 mL) butter
2 tbsp (30 mL) dried basil
2 tsp (10 mL) cracked black peppercorns
2 cups (500 mL) heavy cream (35% m.f.)
salt

Place tomatoes and their juice in a large saucepan and bring to a boil over medium-high heat. Turn off burner and stir in baking soda. Leave on burner about 10 minutes, stirring occasionally until foam rises to the top. Skim.

Return heat to low and add butter, basil and cracked peppercorns. Simmer uncovered 20 minutes, stirring occasionally. Cover saucepan and continue to simmer 1 minute; stir in heavy cream. Remove from burner and let stand 20 minutes. Adjust seasoning, if desired, with salt.

To serve: return to serving temperature and divide between warmed soup bowls.

Serves 6 to 8.

Mulligatawny
Soup

The Baldwins Resort, Windemere, ON

Adapted from the cuisine of southern India, this curry-laced soup is the creation of Chef Janice Goodings, who notes that it may be made with either cooked chicken or lamb.

1 tbsp (15 mL) butter
½ large green pepper, chopped
½ large onion, chopped
1 medium carrot, chopped
1 small apple, peeled, cored and chopped
1 stalk celery, chopped
2 tsp (10 mL) curry powder
4 tsp (20 mL) all-purpose flour
1 large clove garlic, sliced
6 whole cloves
1 tomato, peeled and diced
4 cups (1 L) chicken stock
2 cups (500 mL) cooked chicken or lamb, in
   bite-sized pieces
½ cup (125 mL) whole milk (3.5% m.f.) or light
   cream (18% m.f.)
salt and freshly ground black pepper

Melt butter over medium heat in a heavy-based saucepan and sweat pepper, onion, carrot, apple and celery until tender. Sprinkle with curry powder and flour. Using a small square of cheesecloth tie garlic and cloves into a bag and add to soup along with tomato and chicken stock. Bring to a boil; reduce heat to simmer and cook until vegetables are tender. Remove spice bag.

Stir in meat and milk or cream; season to taste with salt and freshly ground black pepper and return to serving temperature, being careful not to boil.

Serves 4 to 6.

Creamy Tomato
Soup

The Epicurean Restaurant & Bistro, Niagara-on-the-Lake, ON

This is just the type of recipe we love to receive. Chef John Pekka Woods has created a winner; his soup is simple to prepare and delicately delicious. Make it with fresh vine-ripened tomatoes when they are in season. When they are not, substitute good-quality canned crushed tomatoes.

2 tbsp (30 mL) olive oil
1 medium sweet onion, thinly sliced
4 cloves garlic, minced
½ tsp (2 mL) salt
4 cups (1 L) peeled and diced tomatoes
  (optional 28 oz/800 g canned crushed
  tomatoes)
½ tsp (2 mL) black pepper
1 tsp (5 mL) Dijon mustard
1 ½ cups (375 mL) heavy cream (35% m.f.)

Heat oil in a heavy-based saucepan over medium heat and add onion, garlic and salt. Cook, stirring frequently until soft and beginning to caramelize, about 10 minutes. Add tomatoes, pepper and mustard; bring to a simmer, cover loosely and cook 20 minutes, stirring occasionally. Cool slightly.

In a blender, purée soup in batches until smooth and creamy. Return to saucepan, whisk in cream and adjust seasoning.

To serve: ladle into warmed bowls. Accompany with your choice of crackers, bread and cheese.

Serves 4 to 6.

Tomato Orange Soup
with Gin

Some might think the combination of tomato and orange, two acidic ingredients, would give this soup an overpowering finish. The secret is to add a splash of gin, which cuts the acid and enhances the natural sweetness of the tomatoes.

This soup has been a favourite at our table for many years and we have had countless requests for the recipe. If sweet vine-ripened tomatoes are not available you may substitute canned Italian tomatoes.

3 tbsp (45 mL) extra virgin olive oil
1 large sweet onion, chopped (Vidalia, Mayan, Walla Walla, etc.)
2 cloves garlic, minced
2 lb (1 kg) sweet vine-ripened tomatoes, peeled and diced
2 ½ cups (625 mL) chicken stock
juice of 2 oranges
1 tbsp (15 mL) chopped fresh basil (1 tsp/5 mL dried)
1 tsp (5 mL) chopped fresh thyme (½ tsp/2 mL dried)
zest of 2 oranges
¼ cup (60 mL) heavy cream (35% M.F.)
2 tbsp (30 mL) gin (optional vodka)
salt

Heat oil in a large, heavy-based saucepan over medium heat. Add onion and garlic, reduce heat to low, then cover and cook until translucent, about 8 to 10 minutes.

Add tomatoes, stock, orange juice, basil and thyme; bring to a simmer and cook, stirring occasionally, until tomatoes are fully cooked and broken down, about 20 minutes. Cool slightly.

In a blender, purée soup in batches until smooth and creamy. Return to saucepan, whisk in orange zest, cream and gin. Adjust seasoning with salt.

Return to serving temperature.

To serve: pour soup into warmed soup bowls. Garnish with a basil leaf.

Serves 4.

Insalata per l'Autunno
(Autumn Salad)

La Perla, Dartmouth, NS

First you will be struck by the unique ingredients in this warm salad and then surprised by its wonderful taste. Using fresh autumn ingredients, including green tomatoes, Chef James MacDougall has created a winner of a recipe. Serve the salad as a first course or increase the portion and serve as a luncheon dish.

Pancetta is a pork product similar to streaky bacon, but it is not smoked. Generally it is seasoned with salt and peppercorns, rolled and tied.

4 parsnips, peeled
½ small green cabbage
2 medium green tomatoes
3 tbsp (45 mL) olive oil
4 ½ oz (125 g) thinly sliced pancetta
2 tsp (10 mL) superfine sugar*
¼ cup (60 mL) balsamic vinegar
salt and pepper
1 head radicchio, cored and leaves separated
Candied Walnuts (recipe follows)

Shave parsnips with a vegetable peeler into ribbons, but only until you reach the core on all four sides. Shred cabbage and thinly slice green tomatoes. Reserve vegetables.

Heat oil in a large skillet over medium heat, add pancetta and fry until crispy. Add parsnip, cabbage and green tomatoes to skillet and cook 2 minutes, stirring constantly. Add sugar and vinegar, reduce heat to low and cook until vegetables soften, about 4 to 5 minutes. Adjust seasoning with salt and pepper.

To serve: place 3 radicchio leaves in centre of each plate. With a slotted spoon, portion tomato mixture between plates in centre of radicchio. Drizzle remaining balsamic liquid from skillet over each salad. Garnish with Candied Walnuts.

*Make your own superfine or caster sugar by processing regular granulated white sugar in a food processor for a few minutes or until the crystals are smaller.

Serves 6 as a first course salad or 4 as a luncheon dish.

Candied Walnuts
8 oz (225 g) walnut halves
1 egg white, lightly beaten
3 oz (85 g) superfine sugar

Preheat oven to 250°F (120°C). In a bowl combine walnuts and egg white; toss to coat. Spread nuts on a baking sheet and sprinkle with sugar. Bake in oven until dry, about 15 to 20 minutes. Cool.

Autumn
Salad

Castle Rock Country Inn, Ingonish Ferry, NS

With its combination of colours, this salad is almost too beautiful to eat! As a final touch, the chef at Castle Rock finishes his salad plate with a fresh pansy blossom.

2 heads romaine lettuce, washed and torn
2 cups (500 mL) cherry tomatoes
8 oz (225 g) mushrooms, cleaned and sliced
1 small can (284 mL) mandarin orange
    segments, drained
3 ½ oz (100 g) shelled sunflower seeds
3 ½ oz (100 g) dried cranberries
freshly grated Parmesan cheese, as garnish
Vinaigrette (recipe follows)

To serve: divide lettuce between chilled salad plates. Arrange cherry tomatoes, mushroom slices and mandarin orange segments decoratively over lettuce. Sprinkle with sunflower seeds and dried cranberries. Drizzle with vinaigrette and sprinkle with grated Parmesan cheese.

Serves 4 to 6.

Vinaigrette
½ cup (125 mL) extra virgin olive oil
2 ½ tbsp (37 mL) balsamic vinegar
2 ½ tbsp (37 mL) apple juice
¾ tsp (4 mL) Italian spices
¼ tsp (1 mL) salt
¼ tsp (1 mL) pepper

Place all ingredients in a bowl and whisk until emulsified. This dressing may be made several hours ahead of time and stored in a sealed jar. Do not refrigerate.

Heirloom Tomato and Sweet Onion Salad
with Balsamic Syrup and Basil Oil

Bishop's Restaurant, Vancouver, BC

The motto at Bishop's Restaurant is to buy from regional farmers and local farm markets to ensure only the freshest prime produce graces the menu. The heirloom tomatoes used in this recipe are the "crème de la crème" of the tomato garden and prized for their flavour, texture and colour.

The balsamic syrup and basil oil should be made in advance. This recipe is shared from the restaurateur's cookbook, *Simply Bishop's* (Douglas and McIntyre, 2003).

1 cup (250 mL) balsamic vinegar
1 tbsp (15 mL) salt
1 cup (250 mL) fresh basil leaves, packed
½ cup (125 mL) olive oil
1 lb (500 g) assorted heirloom tomatoes
1 sweet onion (Vidalia, Walla Walla, Mayan, etc.)
sea salt and freshly ground pepper

Heat balsamic vinegar in a small saucepan over medium heat. Bring to a boil, reduce heat to a simmer and cook, uncovered, until reduced to ¼ cup (60 mL). Cool to room temperature and place in a squeeze bottle. Refrigerate until needed. Syrup will keep 2 to 3 weeks refrigerated.

Fill a medium saucepan with water, add salt and bring to a boil over medium heat. Blanch basil leaves by plunging into boiling water 1 to 2 minutes, then immediately drain in a colander under cold running water. Squeeze leaves to remove excess water. In a blender or food processor, combine basil and olive oil and process until mixture is puréed and a brilliant green colour. Transfer to a covered container and refrigerate until needed. Oil will keep 4 to 5 days. Before serving bring to room temperature and shake well before applying.

Slice or quarter tomatoes according to size. Slice onion as thinly as possible.

To serve: arrange tomatoes attractively on plates and top with onion slices. Drizzle with balsamic syrup and basil oil. Season to taste with sea salt and pepper.

Serves 6.

Caprese
Salad

Resembling the stripes of the Italian national flag, this colourful red, white and green salad touches your palate with Mediterranean flavours.

We like to make our salad with fresh buffalo bocconcini mozzarella that today is made from a combination of water buffalo and cow's milk. If buffalo mozzarella is unavailable, use the regular cow's milk variety.

Balsamic Reduction (recipe follows)
1 lb (500 g) vine-ripened Roma tomatoes, sliced
salt and pepper
6 balls buffalo bocconcini mozzarella cheese,
  sliced
fresh basil leaves, chopped
4 to 5 tbsp (60-75 mL) extra virgin olive oil

Prepare balsamic reduction in advance.

To serve: on each plate arrange tomato slices in a circle and season lightly with salt and pepper. Top tomatoes with mozzarella slices. Garnish with fresh basil. Drizzle balsamic reduction over salad and encircle with a line of olive oil.

Serves 4 to 6.

Balsamic Reduction
¾ cup (175 mL) balsamic vinegar
½ tsp (2 mL) granulated sugar

In a saucepan over medium heat, stir vinegar with sugar. Cook, stirring frequently until reduced to ¼ cup (60 mL). Cool and refrigerate until ready to use. Bring to room temperature before serving.

Makes ¼ cup (60 mL).

Prawns in Coconut Masala, p.44

Luncheon

This array of luncheon recipes includes dishes that can also be served as appetizers if portioned in smaller amounts or form part of a buffet if amounts are increased. We simply suggest you read the ingredient lists and decide how much to prepare.

Meeru Dhalwala of renowned Vij's Restaurant in Vancouver says that Prawns in Coconut Masala can also be passed around with drinks. We found that the Tomato Chèvre Tartlet from Rhubarb Café & Grill and the Garrison House Inn's Ratatouille Niçoise serve equally well as side dishes to meat and seafood entrées.

Red
Flatbread

Suede Lounge, Edmonton, AB

Chef Jon Setterland names his flatbread/pizza dishes by a colour that corresponds to the ingredients. Green features a curry base; white, a pear and Gorgonzola base; and black, a cumin and black bean base. Here he shares with us his Red Flatbread recipe with its delicious basil-tomato salsa base.

Be sure to prepare the pizza dough and roasted garlic in advance.

Pizza Dough (recipe follows)
4 cloves Roasted Garlic, minced (recipe follows)
1 tsp (5 mL) extra virgin olive oil
2 large vine ripe tomatoes, seeded and cut into fine dice
handful fresh basil leaves, rough-chopped
½ cup (125 mL) thinly sliced peaches (drain well if using canned)
6 to 8 slices prosciutto
salt and pepper
4 oz (125 g) shredded mozzarella cheese

Preheat oven to 450°F (230°C). Roll out pizza dough in desired shape (rectangle or round) to a thickness of ¾ in (2 cm); lightly brush with olive oil. Evenly distribute garlic, tomatoes, basil, peaches and prosciutto over dough. Season with salt and pepper and sprinkle with mozzarella.

Move flatbread to a baking sheet or directly onto a preheated baking stone.

Bake until crust is golden brown and cheese is bubbly, about 12 minutes and cut into serving portions.

Makes one 14-inch (35-cm) pizza.

Pizza Dough
1 package active dry yeast (¼ oz/7 g)
1 ¾ cups (425 mL) all-purpose flour, portioned, plus additional flour for kneading
¾ cup (175 mL) warm water (110°F/44°C), divided (to be consistent with other recipes)
1 tsp (5 mL) salt
1 tsp (5 mL) olive oil

In a small bowl whisk together yeast, 1 tbsp (15 mL) flour and ¼ cup (60 mL) warm water. Let stand in a draft-free area until surface begins to bubble, about 5 minutes.

In a large bowl, combine salt and 1 ½ cups (375 mL) flour. Stir yeast mixture, add to flour along with oil and remaining warm water and stir until smooth. Stir in enough of the remaining flour until dough pulls away from the sides of the bowl.

Flour a dry surface, add dough and knead, adding additional flour as necessary, until dough

is smooth and elastic, about 6 to 8 minutes. Form into a ball, roll in additional flour and enclose in plastic wrap. Refrigerate up to 2 hours before rolling into pizza.

Makes a 14-inch (35-cm) pizza round.

Roasted Garlic
1 whole garlic bulb
1 tsp (5 mL) olive oil

Preheat oven to 350°F (180°C). Rub loose skin from garlic bulb. Trim root end flat and snip tip end from each clove; be careful not to detach individual cloves. Set bulb on a sheet of aluminum foil and drizzle oil over it. Enclose bulb with foil and place in oven. Roast until soft, about 1 hour.

Unwrap garlic, cool slightly and squeeze out individual cloves through the cut end. Unused cloves may be refrigerated for later use.

Tomato Chèvre
Tartlet

Rhubarb Café & Grill, Indian Point, NS

Chef Paul MacInnis serves this tartlet with grilled asparagus as a vegetarian dish or as a side accompaniment to lamb entrées. He suggests that you find tomatoes similar in size to the diameter of your ramekins, and he cautions that if you are unable to find very tiny potatoes, reduce the quantity and cut the potatoes to make 4 pieces per ramekin.

The tarts can be prepared up to 24 hours in advance: just cover the ramekins with plastic wrap and refrigerate. Bring to room temperature before baking.

4 large tomatoes
salt and pepper, portioned
12 baby red potatoes
¼ cup (60 mL) olive oil, portioned
1 ½ tsp (7 mL) dried rosemary, crushed
1 medium red onion, thinly sliced
1 tbsp (15 mL) balsamic vinegar
1 tsp (5 mL) granulated sugar
8 oz (250 g) chèvre cheese
¼ cup (60 mL) dried bread crumbs
2 tsp (10 mL) fresh thyme leaves
2 cloves garlic, thinly sliced
3 or 4 kalamata olives, thinly sliced
puff pastry sheets
thyme sprigs for garnish

Preheat oven to 325°F (160°C). Split tomatoes in half, season with salt and pepper and roast 60 minutes. Peel skins, remove seeds and pour off juices. Reserve.

Cut potatoes in half, place in a saucepan with cold water; bring to a boil, then reduce heat to medium and cook until just tender. Drain. In a bowl, combine 1 tbsp (15 mL) olive oil, rosemary, salt and pepper. Add potato pieces and toss to coat. Reserve.

To caramelize onions, heat 1 tsp (5 mL) olive oil in a heavy-based skillet over high heat, add onion and sauté, stirring constantly. Slow the browning process by adding water to the skillet, ¼ cup (60 mL) at a time, allowing it to evaporate before adding more. Cook in this manner 12 minutes, then stir in balsamic vinegar and sugar. Deglaze with water one last time and cook until onions are sticky and syrupy. Reserve.

For the cheese filling, in a bowl mix together chèvre, breadcrumbs and thyme. Season with pepper and reserve.

Preheat oven to 400°F (200°C). Cut puff pastry into 6 circles large enough to cover the inside of the ramekin, but not so large as to protrude over the edge.

Grease each ramekin with olive oil. Place one sliver of garlic and three slices of olive in the bottom of each. Add tomato in a single layer, lining the entire ramekin. If you make a break in the tomato, patch it with another small piece so it will not leak when the cheese melts.

Layer chèvre cheese mixture on tomatoes and top with caramelized onion. Arrange potato pieces on top of onion, pressing them down to just below the rim of the ramekin. Top with a puff pastry round and gently seal the edge.

Bake tarts until pastry is browned, about 10 to 15 minutes. Remove from oven and let stand 5 minutes.

To serve: using a thin knife, loosen tart from the side of the ramekin. Hold ramekin with an oven mitt, place a serving plate on top and quickly invert and gently remove ramekin. Garnish tart with a sprig of thyme, and repeat for each tart. Accompany with seasonal vegetable of choice.

Serves 6.

Tomato Belle Tart
with Basil Purée

The Epicurean Restaurant & Bistro, Niagara-on-the-Lake, ON

This recipe works well either as individual tart servings or as one large tart. At the restaurant the tarts are made with Belle cheese, a local fresh soft chèvre. Chef Woods comments that, if specialty cheeses are not always available in your area, any variety of creamy goat or cow's milk cheese can be used in the recipe.

1 tbsp (15 mL) olive oil
1 small onion, sliced, rings separated
8 oz (250 g) Belle cheese at room temperature (optional creamed chèvre or cow's milk cheese)
1 Tart Shell (recipe follows)
1 ½ cups (375 mL) thinly sliced teardrop or grape tomatoes
Basil Purée (recipe follows)

Preheat oven to 375°F (190°C). Heat olive oil in a heavy skillet over high heat. Add onion, stir constantly and cook until caramelized, softened and golden brown. Remove from heat.

Spread cheese over the bottom of tart shell and top with caramelized onion and tomato slices. Drizzle with basil purée. Heat in oven 5 minutes to warm.

Serves 4.

Tart Shell

1 ¾ cups (425 mL) all-purpose flour
½ tsp (2 mL) salt
½ cup (125 mL) unsalted butter, cold and diced
1 egg
1 tbsp (15 mL) cold water

Combine flour and salt in the bowl of a food processor fitted with a metal blade. Pulse to combine. Add butter and egg and process for a few seconds. Sprinkle with water and process a few seconds longer until dough just combines.

Wrap in plastic wrap and refrigerate 30 minutes. Roll to ⅛-in (30-mm) thickness and transfer to a 10-in (25-cm) tart pan with removable bottom. Cover and cool in freezer 30 minutes.

Preheat oven to 350°F (180°C). Prick shell all over with a fork and blind bake (line shell with foil or parchment paper and fill with dried beans or ceramic pie weights) 15 minutes. Remove weights and liner and continue to bake until golden brown, about 5 minutes longer. Remove from oven and cool.

Basil Purée

1 large bunch fresh basil, leaves and tender
   stalks only
a few drops extra virgin olive oil
salt

Bring a saucepan of water to a boil and plunge
basil 4 seconds. Drain and immediately add to
an ice bath to stop cooking process and keep
basil bright green. Remove from ice bath and
squeeze dry.

Chop basil, add to a blender and purée with just
enough olive oil to get mixture 'turning' in the
blender. Season purée with salt and store in a
refrigerator up to 1 week.

39

Vine-Ripened Tomato
and Balsamic Bruschetta

Stanhope Beach Resort, Stanhope, PE

Try this easy appetizer when your garden is overflowing with ripe tomatoes. At the Stanhope Bay Resort, Chef Victor MacLean uses both red and yellow tomatoes and adds a touch of lime juice and honey.

1 small baguette
3 vine-ripened tomatoes, chopped
1 large clove garlic, minced
2 tbsp (30 mL) diced red onion
2 green onions, white and light green parts, diced
zest and juice of ½ lime,
1 tbsp (15 mL) liquid honey
2 tbsp (30 mL) balsamic vinegar
1 ½ tbsp (22 mL) extra virgin olive oil
salt and pepper
shaved Asiago cheese, as garnish

Preheat oven to 325°F (160°C). Slice baguette on the bias into ¾-inch (2-cm) ovals. Arrange slices on a baking sheet and bake until lightly browned, about 15 minutes. Reserve.

Combine tomatoes, garlic and red and green onions in a bowl. In a separate bowl whisk together lime juice and zest, honey, vinegar and olive oil. Pour over tomatoes and stir to combine. Season with salt and pepper and refrigerate 1 hour, covered, to allow flavours to blend.

To serve: preheat oven to 350°F (180°C). Using a slotted spoon, ladle tomato mixture onto toast rounds. Sprinkle with Asiago cheese and bake until cheese starts to melt, about 5 to 10 minutes.

Serves 4.

Ratatouille
Niçoise

The Garrison House Inn, Annapolis Royal, NS

Ratatouille just begs to be made when late summer approaches and gardens are abundant with fresh tomatoes, eggplant and zucchini. This recipe is easily doubled or tripled — just lower the amount of olive oil, as you do not need to increase it in the same proportion. If you prepare extra, simply portion servings in freezer bags or containers and store in your freezer. Ratatouille also makes a nice side-dish accompaniment for meat and seafood entrées.

1 eggplant, about 2 lb (1 kg)
⅓ cup (75 mL) extra virgin olive oil, portioned
1 lb (500 g) onion, chopped
1 ½ tbsp (22 mL) minced garlic
6 large vine-ripened tomatoes, cut into wedges
2 red peppers, seeded and cut into ½-in (1-cm) squares
3 cups (750 mL) tender zucchini, cut into ½-inch (1-cm) cubes
2 cups (500 mL) grated melting cheese (parmigiano-reggiano, pecorino, etc.)
1 cup (250 mL) bread crumbs

Preheat broiler. Trim eggplant and cut into ½-in (1-cm) slices lengthwise. Lightly brush both sides with olive oil and place on a baking sheet. Broil until lightly browned on one side, flip and broil the other side, about 10 minutes total. Cool slightly and cut into cubes.

Heat remaining oil in a large, heavy-based saucepan over low heat. Add onion and garlic and sweat until softened, about 10 minutes. Add tomatoes, raise heat to simmer and cook 3 to 4 minutes until tomatoes begin to break down.

Add eggplant, red pepper and zucchini and cook, covered, over low heat, stirring occasionally until vegetables are soft and flavours blended, about 1 hour. Uncover and continue cooking to reduce liquid to desired consistency.

Preheat broiler again. In a bowl combine cheese and breadcrumbs. Pour vegetable mixture into a lightly buttered ovenproof casserole and top with cheese mixture. Place under broiler and cook until cheese has melted and top is bubbly.

To serve: portion ratatouille on serving plates. Accompany with tossed salad and fresh warm bread.

Serves 4 to 6.

Grape Tomato
Clafouti

Grape tomatoes turn a traditional sweet cherry clafouti into a savoury luncheon treat. The concentrated sweet flavour of these tiny tomatoes is the perfect complement to the clafouti's fresh herbs and cheese.

2 cups (500 mL) grape tomatoes
¼ cup (60 mL) sliced black olives
2 green onions, sliced
2 tbsp (30 mL) extra virgin olive oil
½ tsp (2 mL) each, chopped fresh thyme and
    rosemary
2 cloves garlic, minced
½ tsp (2 mL) granulated sugar
pinch salt and pepper
1 cup (250 mL) light cream (18% m.f.)
3 whole eggs
2 tbsp (30 mL) all-purpose flour
2 cups (500 mL) grated melting cheese of choice
    (mozzarella, Manchego, Swiss, etc.)

Preheat oven to 400°F (200°C). Spread tomatoes, olives and green onions in a shallow 6-cup (1.5-L) baking dish. Drizzle with olive oil and sprinkle with herbs, garlic, sugar, salt and pepper. Bake until tomatoes begin to shrivel, about 10 minutes. Remove from oven and reduce oven temperature to 350°F (180°C).

In a bowl combine light cream, eggs and flour and whisk until smooth.

Pour egg mixture over tomatoes and sprinkle with cheese. Return to oven and bake until golden and puffed, about 30 minutes.

To serve: portion clafouti on individual serving plates. Accompany with salad and fresh baked goods.

Serves 4 to 6.

Prawns in Coconut
Masala

Vij's, Vancouver, BC

Ever conscious of the environment from which Vij's obtains its ingredients, the chef notes that the restaurant tries to use wild North American prawns. If wild prawns are unavailable they choose California farmed prawns, shying away from tiger prawns farmed in Asia, where the farming practices are considered highly questionable by organizations monitoring healthy or sustainable seafood. This recipe is shared from *Vij's Elegant and Inspired Indian Cuisine* (Douglas and McIntyre, 2006).

30 prawns, shelled and de-veined (16 to 20 count)
2 tsp (10 mL) salt, portioned
2 tbsp (30 mL) ghee* or canola oil
½ tsp (2 mL) cumin seeds
2 large onions, diced
3 large tomatoes, finely chopped
2 tbsp (30 mL) coconut milk, well stirred
2 tbsp (30 mL) red wine vinegar
2 tsp (10 mL) chopped green chilies
3 bunches green onions, white and green parts, chopped

Place prawns in a colander and rinse under cold running water. Drain well and place in a bowl; sprinkle with 1 tsp (5 mL) salt. Cover with plastic wrap and set aside in the refrigerator while you prepare the coconut masala.

In a large skillet melt ghee or oil on medium-high heat 1 minute. Add cumin seeds and allow them to sizzle 30 seconds. Add onions, reduce heat slightly and sauté 5 to 8 minutes, stirring often until golden brown. Be careful not to burn onions.

Stir in tomatoes, coconut milk, vinegar, chilies and remaining 1 tsp (5 mL) salt. Cook 5 minutes or until tomatoes have broken down. Add green onions and stir well. Add prawns, stirring constantly until they become pinkish-orange, about 3 minutes. Immediately remove from the heat.

To serve: divide coconut masala between 6 small plates and top each serving with five prawns.

Serves 6.

* Ghee is an Indian form of clarified butter with a nutty, caramel aroma and flavour.

Smoked Tomato Lobster
Brûlée

Dayboat, Oyster Bed Bridge, PE

If you live in the Garden of the Gulf, as does Chef Sean Furlong at Dayboat, you have no problem finding fresh local seafood and produce. Nothing tastes finer than lobster straight from the wharf, succulent homegrown tomatoes and newly harvested Prince Edward Island potatoes.

Smoked Tomato Shells (recipe follows)
Pesto Mayonnaise (recipe follows)
8 small new potatoes
meat from 1 x 1-lb (500-g) lobster, cut into bite-sized pieces
½ avocado, peel and stone removed, cubed
1 green onion, sliced on a bias
zest of ½ lemon
salt and pepper
6 oz (170 g) mascarpone cheese
mixed salad greens

Prepare Smoked Tomato Shells and Pesto Mayonnaise.

Add whole, unpeeled potatoes to a saucepan of cold, salted water. Bring to a boil and cook until barely tender, about 5 to 10 minutes, depending on size. Drain and cool. Cut each potato into 8 pieces.

In a bowl, gently combine lobster, potato, avocado, green onion, lemon zest and enough Pesto Mayonnaise to moisten well. Adjust seasoning with salt and pepper.

Preheat broiler. Arrange tomato shells on a baking sheet. Portion lobster mixture into shells and top with mascarpone cheese. Broil until cheese is lightly coloured but interior is still cool, about 1 minute.

To serve: portion salad greens on 4 serving plates and centre tomatoes on greens.

Serves 4.

Smoked Tomato Shells
4 large vine-ripened tomatoes
1 cup (250 mL) seasoned, commercial wood chips (hickory, apple, mesquite, etc.)

Place wood chips in a foil container, cover with water and soak 30 minutes. Drain water from wood chips. Using a sharp knife, pierce the bottom of the container in at least 8 places.

Remove the grill rack from one side of a gas grill and place the container of chips on the coals. Turn the burners to high heat, cover the grill and let the chips smoke 10 minutes.

While the chips are smoking prepare tomatoes. Fill a large bowl halfway with cold water and ice cubes. Bring a large saucepan of water to a boil and immerse tomatoes 10 to 15 seconds. Immediately refresh tomatoes in the ice water bath to stop the cooking process; remove tomatoes and slide off the skins. Cut "lids" from tomatoes and remove seeds and pulp, being careful not to puncture the sides.

On the grill, turn the heat to medium on the side with the chips and turn the other side off. Arrange tomato shells in a grillproof pan and set on the remaining grilling rack; close the lid and smoke 8 to 10 minutes.

Pesto Mayonnaise
small handful of fresh basil leaves
1 tsp (5 mL) olive oil
1 tsp (5mL) minced garlic
½ cup (125 mL) egg-based mayonnaise
fresh lemon juice
salt and pepper

In a food processor, combine basil, oil and garlic; process to a purée. Add mayonnaise and pulse to emulsify. Adjust seasoning to taste with lemon juice, salt and pepper.

Makes ½ cup (125 mL).

Medusa
Mussels

Flex Mussels, Charlottetown, PE

Flex Mussels rightly boasts that all its mussel dishes have a unique flavour. This recipe, featuring fresh tomato with a hint of oregano and permeated with lemon zest, is a winner.

Chef Garner Quain comments that the key to making great mussels is speed. Using high heat and a short cooking time, you prevent overcooking. Have all your ingredients ready and don't overload the pot with mussels. If you are cooking a large quantity consider making several smaller batches.

2 to 3 lb (1-1.5 kg) fresh mussels
1 tsp (5 mL) olive oil
1 tsp (5 mL) minced garlic
1 large vine-ripened tomato, chopped
zest of 1 lemon
2 sprigs fresh oregano
½ cup (125 mL) white wine
½ cup (125 mL) crumbled feta cheese
crusty baguette, sliced

Scrub and debeard mussels, discarding any that do not close when lightly tapped or have broken shells. Reserve.

Heat oil in a large, heavy-based saucepan over medium-high heat. Add garlic, tomato, lemon zest and oregano and sauté, stirring frequently until tomatoes begin to break down, about 2 minutes.

Deglaze the pan with wine, stirring with a wooden spoon and gently scraping the bottom of the saucepan to combine all the ingredients. Cook 1 minute. Add mussels, cover and bring to a boil. Cook 4 to 6 minutes, stirring midway, until all mussels are open. Remove cover and allow sauce to reduce by one-third or until desired consistency.

To serve: using a slotted spoon, remove mussels to a warm serving dish, discarding any that did not fully open. Sprinkle feta cheese over mussels and top with reduced sauce. Serve immediately with lots of fresh, sliced baguette.

Serves 4.

Pan Fried Scallops
and Artichoke Purée

Le Château Bonne Entente, Ste. Foy, QC

Executive Chef Marie-Chantal Lepage of Château Bonne Entente presents this stunning luncheon dish featuring vine-ripened Bella or Campari tomatoes and caviar from freshwater sturgeon of northern Quebec's Abitibi region.

14 oz (398 mL) precooked artichoke bottoms, drained
1 garlic clove, minced
2 tsp (10 mL) lemon juice
few drops olive oil, divided
sea salt and freshly ground pepper, portioned
4 Bella or Campari tomatoes, sliced lengthwise
leaves from 2 sprigs fresh thyme
1 cup (250 mL) white wine
3 tbsp (45 mL) fish stock
1 ½ tbsp (22 mL) chopped scallions
1 ⅓ cups (325 mL) heavy cream (35% m.f.)
few drops fresh lemon juice
8 sprigs Italian parsley
1 lb (500 g) extra large sea scallops (8 count)
2 tsp (10 mL) Abitibi caviar

Purée artichoke bottoms and garlic in a food processor. With motor running add lemon juice and a few drops of olive oil until mixture thickens. Adjust seasoning with salt and pepper, cover with plastic wrap and set aside.

Preheat oven to 350°F (180°C). Arrange sliced tomatoes on a baking pan and sprinkle with a few drops of olive oil and fresh thyme leaves and season with salt and pepper. Roast tomatoes until softened, about 10 to 15 minutes. Set aside and keep warm.

In a large saucepan over medium-high heat reduce wine, fish stock and scallions until liquid has almost evaporated. Stir in heavy cream and reduce until consistency is syrupy, about 10 minutes. Keep warm. Just prior to serving stir in a few drops of fresh lemon juice.

Using a little olive oil, lightly fry Italian parsley and set aside. Using the same skillet adjust heat to high and quickly sear scallops, turning once.

To serve: spoon two small mounds of artichoke purée on each of 4 serving plates. Top each mound of purée with a tomato half, a parsley sprig and a seared scallop. Drizzle with warm sauce and sprinkle with caviar.

Serves 4.

Unclassic Shrimp
Cocktail

Stone Road Grille, Niagara-on-the-Lake, ON

Tomatillos are also known as Mexican green tomatoes. Wasabi, a common ingredient in Japanese cookery, has a pungent, fiery flavour and will produce a vibrant green sauce.

24 shrimp, cooked, peeled and de-veined
½ cup Green Tomato Cocktail Sauce (recipe follows)
½ lime, quartered, as garnish

To serve: position a dish of green tomato cocktail sauce on a tray of crushed ice. Arrange shrimp around sauce. Garnish plate with lime wedges.

Serves 4.

Green Tomato Cocktail Sauce

¼ lb (125 g) tomatillo or small green tomatoes
1 ½ tbsp (22 mL) minced red onion
1 tsp (5 mL) jalapeño pepper, seeded and diced
1 tbsp (15 mL) fresh lime juice
1 ½ tbsp (22 mL) extra virgin olive oil
1 ½ tbsp (22 mL) fresh grated wasabi root or 2 tsp (10 mL) wasabi powder
¼ bunch cilantro, washed and stemmed

If using tomatillos, remove parchment-like covering, rinse and chop. If using green tomatoes wash, remove stem end and chop. Combine tomatoes, onion, pepper, lime juice, olive oil and wasabi in a blender and purée. Add cilantro and pulse to combine.

Makes ⅔ cup.

Puttanesca, p.74

Main Course

In this section the star of our show — the tomato — highlights lamb, chicken, seafood and vegetarian offerings. The dishes are innovative and represent the best regional ingredients from across the country. Youvetsi, a dish from Opa Taverna in Halifax and Mediterranean Braised Lamb Shanks from Chef Paul MacInnis in Indian Point, Nova Scotia, feature succulent lamb that will melt in your mouth. Two of the chefs from Ontario showed a partiality for vegetarian sauces and responded with Rigatoni with Tomato, Basil and Mushroom Sauce and Puttanesca Sauce.

Whether you are a beginner or seasoned cook, you will find numerous recipes in this section suited to your level of expertise. Many are ideal for weekday family meals while others are perfect for entertaining.

Chicken
à la Edge

Edgewater Lodge, Whistler, BC

Sun-dried tomatoes add an intense burst of tomato flavour as you bite into this succulent baked chicken dish from the kitchen of Chef Thomas Piekarski. Use sun-dried tomatoes that are not packed in oil in this recipe. If you are unable to find them, use the oil-packed variety and remove the oil with paper towels before slicing.

4 boneless, skinless chicken breasts
1 small round Camembert cheese
1 ½ tbsp (22 mL) chopped pistachio nuts
½ cup (125 mL) thinly sliced sun-dried tomatoes
1 tbsp (15 mL) chopped fresh thyme (or 1 tsp/
   5 mL dried)
salt and pepper
1 egg
2 tsp (10 mL) water
pinch each salt, pepper and paprika
¾ cup (175 mL) all-purpose flour
2 cups (500 mL) soft breadcrumbs
⅓ cup (75 mL) vegetable oil
⅓ cup (75 mL) butter
Basil Pesto (recipe follows)
4 lemon wedges

Place chicken breasts between 2 layers of waxed paper and pound with a chef's mallet until evenly flat and wrapable. On the centre of each breast place one-quarter of the cheese, pistachio nuts, sun-dried tomatoes and thyme and season with salt and pepper. Gently fold each breast in half into a package, pressing edges to adhere. Remove to a baking sheet, cover and refrigerate 2 hours.

Preheat oven to 375° F (190°C). In a bowl, beat egg, water, salt, pepper and paprika to make an egg wash. Dredge chicken packages in flour, dip in egg wash and coat with breadcrumbs, pressing to adhere.

Heat oil and butter in a skillet over medium-high heat and add chicken, keeping the oil level to almost one-third the height of the chicken. Cook, turning once until both sides are golden brown. Remove chicken to an ovenproof pan and bake 15 minutes or until slightly firm when pressed.

To serve: arrange chicken on warmed plates. Accompany with Basil Pesto, vegetables of choice and lemon wedges.

Serves 4.

Basil Pesto

2 handfuls fresh basil, chopped
¼ cup (60 mL) extra virgin olive oil
6 cloves garlic, minced
1 tbsp (15 mL) drained capers
⅓ cup (75 mL) Parmesan cheese
pinch salt and pepper

In a food processor, add all ingredients and process until well combined. Refrigerate unused pesto in a glass jar covered with a thin layer of olive oil to prevent it from turning brown.

Makes ¾ cup (175 mL).

Basil Pesto and Goat Cheese Stuffed Chicken
on Smoked Tomato Risotto

Chives Canadian Bistro, Halifax, NS

Basil and tomato are a classic pairing, but at Chives Canadian Bistro Chef Craig Flinn puts a new twist on the old favourite by accompanying his basil-infused chicken breasts with a risotto delicately flavoured with smoked tomatoes. The browned skin of the chicken enhances both the flavour and appearance of the dish.

6 chicken breasts, boneless, with skin on
½ cup (125 mL) Basil Pesto (see page 57)
¼ cup (60 mL) chèvre (goat's milk cheese)
¼ cup (60 mL) freshly grated Parmesan cheese
2 tbsp (30 mL) heavy cream (35% m.f.)
1 egg
1 tsp (5 mL) sea salt
1 tsp (5 mL) pepper
Smoked Tomato Risotto (recipe follows)

Preheat oven to 425°F (220°C). Rinse and pat dry chicken breasts. Remove the small tenders (strips of rib meat found on the back of each breast), and set aside. Using a boning knife, make a small slit in each breast, forming a pocket.

In a food processor blend chicken tenders, pesto, cheeses, cream and egg until smooth; season with salt and pepper. Using a piping bag fill each pocket with the pesto filling. Bake chicken, skin side up, 12 to 15 minutes or until golden brown and juices run clear.

To serve: arrange chicken breasts on warm serving plates. Accompany with Smoked Tomato Risotto.

Serves 6.

Smoked Tomato Risotto
1 cup (250 mL) seasoned commercial wood
    chips (hickory, apple, etc.)
2 large tomatoes
3 tbsp (45 mL) olive oil
2 cloves garlic, minced
½ cup (125 mL) finely diced onion
1 cup (250 mL) arborio rice
½ cup (125 mL) white wine
4 cups (1 L) chicken stock, heated
½ cup (125 mL) grated Parmesan cheese

Soak wood chips in water 30 minutes. Drain chips and place them on a heavy sheet of aluminum foil. Heat barbecue to high and place wood chips on the coals under the rack; cover until they begin to smoke.

Slice tomatoes in thick slices; arrange them in a grillproof pan and set it on the rack above the wood chips. Reduce heat to medium, lower the lid and smoke tomatoes 5 minutes. Roughly chop them and reserve in a bowl.

In a sauté pan, heat oil over medium heat. Sauté garlic and onion, stirring frequently until softened. Add rice and cook 3 minutes until grains are slightly translucent.

Pour wine into rice and cook, stirring often until liquid has evaporated. Add ½ cup (125 mL) chicken stock and cook, stirring often, then add remaining stock ½ cup (125 mL) at a time, allowing rice to completely absorb liquid each time, about 18 to 20 minutes or until rice is almost tender. Add chopped smoked tomatoes and Parmesan cheese. Allow risotto to rest 5 minutes before serving.

Youvetsi

Opa Taverna, Halifax, NS

Owner Costa Elles comments that this lamb-and-tomato-based traditional Greek dish is one of the most popular entrées at the restaurant, and we understand why. It exudes the aromas and flavours of warm Mediterranean nights, and in Greece is often served at family gatherings or Sunday evening suppers.

The recipe is enhanced with the use of fresh vine-ripened tomatoes, but feel free to use canned tomatoes if vine-ripened are unavailable.

4 tbsp (60 mL) olive oil
2 lb (1 kg) lamb, cut into 2-in (5-cm) cubes
2 large onions, diced
2 bay leaves
2 cinnamon sticks
2 tsp (10 mL) chopped fresh rosemary
½ tsp (2 mL) salt
½ tsp (2 mL) pepper
3 cloves garlic, minced
5 cups (1.25 L) peeled and crushed fresh tomatoes (optional crushed canned tomatoes)
2 tbsp (30 mL) steak sauce (optional 1 ½ tsp/ 7 mL Worcestershire sauce)

¼ cup (60 mL) red wine
1 cup (250 mL) orzo pasta
4 oz (125 g) grated Kefalograviera cheese, or other aged melting cheese
fresh chopped cilantro or parsley, for garnish

Preheat oven to 350°F (180°C). Heat olive oil in a large, heavy, ovenproof saucepan over high heat. Add lamb and sauté, stirring frequently, 5 to 7 minutes. Reduce heat to medium, add onions and cook 3 minutes. Add herbs and seasonings, garlic, tomatoes, steak sauce and red wine to lamb mixture and bring back to a simmer. Cover, place in oven and bake until lamb is tender, about 1 to 1 ½ hours.

During the last 10 minutes of baking time, cook orzo in a large pot of boiling salted water until *al dente*, about 10 minutes. Drain.

Add orzo to lamb mixture and adjust seasoning. Pour lamb into a large casserole dish, top with cheese and bake until cheese melts, about 10 minutes.

To serve: portion into serving dishes. Garnish with chopped cilantro or parsley. Accompany with fresh crusty bread and a Greek salad.

Serves 4 to 6.

Mediterranean Braised
Lamb Shanks

Rhubarb Grill & Café, Indian Point, NS

Chef Paul MacInnis says, if you prefer, char the lamb shanks over the high heat of a grill or barbecue rather than on a stovetop.

4 lamb shanks (about 1 lb/500 g) each
sea salt and freshly ground pepper
all-purpose flour, for dusting
3 tbsp (45 mL) olive oil
1 red onion, chopped
1 stalk celery, chopped
1 leek, white part, chopped
1 large carrot, peeled and chopped
4 garlic cloves, minced
1 cup (250 mL) dry red wine
1 ½ cups (375 mL) diced vine-ripened plum
  tomatoes (optional canned Italian tomatoes)
1 tsp (5 mL) dried thyme
1 tsp (5 mL) dried oregano
1 bay leaf
sea salt and freshly ground pepper, second amount
8 fresh thyme sprigs, portioned

Preheat oven to 250° F (120° C). Trim excess fat from lamb shanks and pat them dry. Season with salt and pepper and toss in all-purpose flour to lightly coat. Heat 2 tbsp (30 mL) oil in a heavy ovenproof braising pot (preferably cast iron) over high heat. Add lamb shanks, in batches if necessary, and quickly brown on all sides. Remove shanks and reserve at room temperature.

Lower heat to medium-high, add remaining oil if necessary and cook aromatics (onion, celery, leek, garlic), adding them one type at a time and stirring each about 1 minute before adding the next. Cook mixture, stirring frequently until caramelized, about 12 to 15 minutes.

Deglaze pot with wine, scraping the bottom to remove pieces of lamb and vegetable into the sauce; cook about 2 to 3 minutes. Add tomatoes, dried thyme, oregano, bay leaf and reserved lamb shanks. Spoon sauce over shanks, cover and place in oven. Bake 3 to 4 hours or until lamb falls off the bone when pushed with the back of a fork.

Gently remove lamb with a slotted spoon, cover and keep warm. Pour liquid from pan through a sieve to remove large pieces. Allow liquid to sit for a few minutes, skim fat and oils from the top and transfer to a new saucepan, discarding the last few tablespoons and the residue that will have sunk to the bottom. Bring to a boil and reduce slightly. Adjust seasoning with salt and pepper.

To serve: place shanks on warmed plates and top with sauce. Garnish with thyme sprigs. Accompany with creamy garlic mashed potatoes and vegetable of choice.

Serves 4.

Bisque
Mussels

Flex Mussels, Charlottetown, PE

We guarantee there will not be a drop of dipping sauce left in the bowl with this fabulous entrée. The rich, creamy brandy sauce will have you searching out fresh mussels at the market just so you can make the recipe again.

The chefs at Flex Mussels comment that when choosing fresh mussels, look for lightly closed shells. Fresh mussels are best eaten the day you buy them, but will last a couple of days in your refrigerator, uncovered, in a container that allows for some drainage.

2 to 3 lb (1 to 1.5 kg) fresh mussels
1 tsp (5 mL) olive oil
1 tsp (5 mL) minced garlic
2 green onions, chopped
1 large vine-ripened tomato, chopped
¼ cup (60 mL) white wine
2 tbsp (30 mL) brandy
½ cup (125 mL) heavy cream (35% m.f.)
4 oz (125 g) cooked lobster meat
2 sprigs fresh thyme
½ lemon
1 crusty baguette, sliced

Scrub and debeard mussels, discarding any that do not close when lightly tapped or have broken shells. Reserve.

Heat oil in a large heavy-based saucepan over medium-high heat. Add garlic, green onion and tomato; sauté, stirring frequently until tomatoes begin to break down, about 2 minutes.

Stir in wine, brandy and cream, and with a wooden spoon gently scrape the bottom of the saucepan to combine all ingredients. Add lobster and cook 1 minute. Add mussels and thyme; cover and bring to a boil. Cook 4 to 6 minutes, stirring midway, until all mussels are open wide. Remove cover and allow sauce to reduce by one-third, or to desired consistency.

To serve: using a slotted spoon, remove mussels to a warm serving dish, discarding any that did not fully open. Squeeze lemon over mussels and pour reduced sauce over all. Serve immediately with lots of fresh bread.

Serves 4.

Mussels with Tomatoes,
Jalapeño and Tequila

Monet's Table, Sarnia, ON

Move over mussels — it's the spicy sauce that's the star of this dish! Remember to have lots of crusty bread on hand for dipping.

1 ½ lb (750 g) fresh mussels
½ cup (125 mL) butter
4 to 5 garlic cloves, minced
¾ cup (175 mL) diced Roma tomatoes
½ cup (125 mL) sliced green onions
½ cup thinly sliced celery
6 x ¼-inch (1-cm) rounds jalapeño pepper, with
    seeds
¼ cup (60 mL) tequila
2 tbsp (30 mL) lime juice, freshly squeezed
salt and pepper, to taste

Scrub and debeard mussels, being careful to discard any that are open or have broken shells. Set aside.

Melt butter in a heavy saucepan over medium-high heat. Add garlic and sauté until fragrant, about 1 minute. Stir in tomatoes, green onions, celery, jalapeño, tequila and lime juice; bring to a boil. Add mussels, cover and steam until mussels open, about 6 minutes. Discard any that do not open.

To serve: using a slotted spoon, transfer mussels to two serving bowls. Simmer sauce, uncovered, until slightly reduced, about 3 minutes. Season with salt and pepper and pour over mussels.

Serves 2.

Blackened Shrimp
with Fresh Tomato Salsa

Inn on the Lake, Waverley, NS

Prepare this salsa when you have an abundant tomato harvest. The salsa is delicious served warm, as it is with shrimp in this recipe. The chef also advises that it is equally tasty served chilled as a dip.

1 ¼ lb (625 g) uncooked jumbo shrimp, peeled and deveined
1 tsp (5 mL) Cajun spice
1 to 2 tsp (5 to 10 mL) vegetable oil
steamed rice, to serve 4
Fresh Tomato Salsa (recipe follows)
parsley sprigs, as garnish

Preheat oven to 350°F (180°C). Rinse shrimp, pat dry and toss with Cajun spice. Heat a heavy, ovenproof skillet over high heat, add oil and sear shrimp 1 minute per side. Finish cooking shrimp in oven, about 5 minutes.

To serve: place shrimp on a bed of steamed rice and top with ¼ cup (60 mL) warm salsa. Garnish with a sprig of fresh parsley.

Serves 4.

Fresh Tomato Salsa

3 cups (750 mL) diced fresh tomatoes, skins and seeds included
¾ cup (175 mL) diced celery
½ cup (125 mL) diced sweet onion
1 tbsp (15 mL) salt
¼ cup (60 mL) granulated sugar
¼ cup (60 mL) white vinegar
1 ½ tbsp (22 mL) mustard seeds
½ green pepper, diced
½ red pepper, diced
3 tbsp (45 mL) tomato paste
2 tbsp (30 mL) diced jalapeño pepper (optional)

Combine tomatoes, celery, onion and salt in a bowl and let sit, covered and refrigerated overnight. The next morning, drain the accumulated liquid and rinse several times with cold water. Place mixture in a large saucepan and stir in sugar, vinegar and mustard seeds. Bring to a boil, reduce heat and simmer 45 minutes, stirring often. Remove from heat.

Stir in green and red peppers, tomato paste and jalapeño pepper. Reheat to a simmer and cook, covered, an additional 15 minutes. Keep warm.

Makes 3 cups (750 mL).

Grilled Sockeye Salmon
with Charred Tomato Relish

Bishop's Restaurant, Vancouver, BC

The sockeye salmon harvest runs from mid-May through September and coincides nicely with barbecue season. John Bishop finds sockeye, with its firm flesh, to be perfect for grilling but cautions that you should be careful not to overcook, as it can become dry. And while the barbecue is hot, throw on some ripe tomatoes and red onion: presto, you now have a quick-and-easy smoky sauce to accompany the fish. This recipe is shared from the restaurateur's cookbook, *Simply Bishop's* (Douglas and McIntyre, 2003).

4 to 6 sockeye salmon fillets, 6 oz (170 g) each
1 to 1 ½ tsp (5 to 7 mL) vegetable oil
sea salt and freshly ground black pepper
Charred Tomato Relish (recipe follows)

Preheat grill to high heat. Rub salmon fillets with vegetable oil and season with salt and pepper. Grill 3 to 4 minutes per side, until just cooked.

To serve: place grilled fillets on warmed plates and ladle 2 to 3 tbsp (30 to 45 mL) of Charred Tomato Relish on the side. Accompany with vegetables of choice.

Serves 4 to 6.

Charred Tomato Relish
1 lb (500 g) ripe tomatoes
½ small red onion, cut into ¼-inch (5-mm) slices
sea salt and freshly ground pepper
¼ cup (60 mL) balsamic vinegar
¼ cup (60 mL) olive oil
2 sprigs fresh basil, chopped

Preheat grill to medium heat. Place whole tomatoes on grill and turn continually until well charred on all sides, about 5 to 6 minutes. At the same time, grill onion slices until lightly charred on both sides, about 8 to 10 minutes.

Coarsely chop tomatoes and onion and remove to a bowl. Season mixture with salt and pepper to taste. Add vinegar, olive oil and basil and toss to combine. Cover and reserve 30 minutes at room temperature for the flavours to develop.

Place relish in a blender or food processor and pulse to chop. Relish may be served hot, cold or at room temperature. It will keep, refrigerated, up to 1 week.

Italian Seafood
Stew

The Italian Gourmet, Halifax, NS

An abundant supply of fresh seafood and a love of Italian cuisine marry beautifully in Chef Kate Abato's seafood stew. She notes that the seafood is cooked separately from the stew stock, then combined during the last five minutes of preparation to avoid overcooking the fish. At The Italian Gourmet the stew is served with crusty bread, a side salad and a glass of red vino!

Stew Stock:
1 tbsp (15 mL) olive oil
1 small green pepper, finely chopped
1 small onion, finely chopped
1 clove garlic, crushed
1 cup (250 mL) fish stock
1 cup (250 mL) fruity red wine
1 cup (250 mL) seeded and diced Roma plum
  tomatoes
½ tsp (2 mL) dried Italian seasoning

Seafood:
2 ½ lb (1.25 kg) mixed seafood such as scallops,
  salmon and white fish, cut into 1 ½-inch
  (3.75-cm) pieces
2 tbsp (30 mL) olive oil
1 medium onion, finely chopped

1 clove garlic, crushed
salt and pepper
fresh basil or parsley, as garnish

For the stew stock, heat olive oil in a large skillet over medium heat; sauté green pepper, onion and garlic, stirring frequently, until onions are translucent, about 5 minutes. Add fish stock and wine, reduce heat and simmer 20 minutes, stirring occasionally. Add tomatoes and Italian seasoning; simmer until tomatoes soften and stock is slightly reduced, about 20 minutes. Keep warm.

Rinse and pat dry seafood, cutting into a uniform size. Heat olive oil in a large skillet over medium heat; sauté onion and garlic, stirring frequently until translucent, about 5 minutes. Add all the seafood, being careful to distribute it evenly in the skillet. Cook 3 to 4 minutes on one side, turn gently and cook an additional 2 minutes. Transfer seafood to stew base and simmer 5 minutes. Adjust seasoning with salt and pepper.

To serve: ladle into shallow bowls. Garnish with fresh basil or parsley.

Serves 6.

Louisiana Seafood
Gumbo

MacKinnon-Cann Inn, Yarmouth, NS

A wonderful treat awaits diners at the MacKinnon-Cann Inn where innkeeper/chef Neil Hisgen serves his brother's gumbo recipe, affectionately called "Johnny's Gumbo" on the menu. This southern-inspired dish has become the inn's signature entrée. The gumbo's woodsy flavour comes from filé powder, a seasoning made from the powdered leaves of the sassafras tree.

4 tbsp (60 mL) unsalted butter
½ cup (125 mL) all-purpose flour
1 tbsp (15 mL) filé powder
1 carrot, chopped
½ yellow onion, diced
½ small red onion, diced
2 cloves garlic, minced
1 stalk celery, diced
4 cups (1 L) peeled and chopped vine-ripened
    tomatoes
4 cups (1 L) clam or chicken stock
¼ tsp (2 mL) minced fresh thyme
⅛ tsp (0.5 mL) Old Bay Seasoning
pinch paprika
pinch cayenne pepper
2 tbsp (30 mL) chopped fresh parsley

1 ½ lb (750 g) mixed fresh seafood (peeled
    shrimp, lobster meat, scallops, crawfish tail
    meat, shucked oysters, etc.)
salt and pepper
4 cups (1 L) cooked rice

Melt butter over medium heat in a large, heavy-based saucepan. Whisk in flour and continue to cook while stirring constantly until "roux" turns a dark brown. This procedure will take about 20 minutes and care must be taken to avoid burning the roux. The mixture will appear quite soupy.

Stir in filé powder and continue to cook 2 minutes, stirring constantly. Add carrot, onion, garlic, celery, tomatoes and stock. Bring back to a boil, reduce heat and simmer 15 minutes. Stir in thyme, Old Bay Seasoning, paprika, cayenne pepper and parsley. Add seafood and simmer until fish is just cooked, about 5 to 7 minutes. Adjust seasoning with salt and pepper.

To serve: divide rice between serving bowls and top with gumbo.

Serves 6.

Smoked Fish Cakes
with Tomato Gelée

The Old Orchard Inn and Spa, Wolfville, NS

Smoked haddock, also known as "finnan haddie" is a lightly salted and smoked haddock fillet. At the Old Orchard Inn, Chef Joe Gillis accompanies his fish cakes with cubes of tomato gelée or aspic, adding a colourful touch to the plate.

1 lb (500 g) russet potatoes
1 tbsp (15 mL) butter
1 medium onion, diced
½ cup (125 mL) fresh corn kernels
1 lb (500 g) smoked haddock, deboned and cut
    into bite sized pieces
¼ cup (60 mL) heavy cream (35% m.f.)
1 tsp (5 mL) Cajun spice (or to taste)
freshly ground pepper
all-purpose flour, for dredging
2 large eggs, beaten
2 cups (500 mL) dry bread crumbs
2 to 3 tbsp (30 to 45 mL) vegetable oil
Tomato Gelée (recipe follows)
assorted salad greens

Cook potatoes in a large pot of salted water. Drain, peel and mash. Set aside.

Melt butter in a large skillet over medium heat and sauté onion, corn and haddock pieces about 5 minutes, stirring occasionally. Add cream and Cajun spice and adjust seasoning with cracked pepper. Continue to cook until liquid is reduced by one-half. Remove from burner and fold in prepared potatoes.

Form mixture into eight patties. Dredge fish cakes in flour, shaking off excess. Dip each cake in egg mixture and coat with breadcrumbs. Set on parchment or waxed paper and cover. Refrigerate at least 45 minutes.

Preheat oven to 325°F (160°C). Heat vegetable oil in a heavy-based ovenproof skillet over medium heat and sear fish cakes, turning once. Remove to oven and heat through, about 15 minutes.

To serve: arrange two fish cakes on each serving plate. Spread a few salad greens on plate and top leaves with cubes of tomato gelée.

Serves 4.

Tomato Gelée

2 cups (500 mL) tomato juice, divided
1 envelope gelatin
½ carrot, grated
½ onion, grated
½ English cucumber, grated
salt and pepper

Place ½-cup (125-mL) tomato juice in a bowl and sprinkle with gelatin, stir to combine and set aside 2 to 3 minutes. Heat remaining tomato juice, grated carrot and onion over medium heat until mixture comes to a simmer. Stir in gelatin mixture and heat until gelatin is melted. Set aside to cool. Stir in cucumber and adjust seasoning with salt and pepper. Pour into a 9-inch (23-cm) square glass baking-dish and refrigerate several hours until set. Cut into cubes.

Puttanesca
Sauce

Chez Piggy, Kingston, ON

Not many sauce recipes can be prepared during the time it takes to cook the pasta. Here is one. The creation of Executive Chef Anne Linton, this sauce emphasizes olives over tomatoes yet has a slight sweetness from the raisins. The recipe has been shared from *The Chez Piggy Cookbook* (Firefly, second printing 2000).

¼ cup (60 mL) golden raisins
½ cup (125 mL) pine nuts
¾ to 1 cup (175 to 250 mL) extra virgin olive oil
15 colossal green olives, pitted and chopped
12 kalamata olives, pitted and chopped
3 cloves garlic, chopped
2 anchovies, rinsed and chopped (optional)
pinch cayenne pepper
3 large, ripe tomatoes, seeded and diced
¼ cup (60 mL) capers, drained
2 tbsp (30 mL) fresh parsley or dill, minced
freshly ground black pepper
1 ½ lb (725 g) fresh pasta, cooked *al dente* and
    drained
freshly grated Parmesan cheese, as garnish

Soak raisins in hot water 15 minutes until soft; drain and chop.

Toast pine nuts in a dry skillet over medium heat, shaking often until golden, about 4 minutes.

Heat olive oil over medium heat in a large skillet and stir in raisins, pine nuts, olives, garlic, anchovies, cayenne, tomatoes, capers and herbs. Cook, stirring frequently until tomatoes start to break down and sauce thickens slightly, about 10 minutes. Toss with hot pasta and season with black pepper

To serve: transfer to pasta bowls. Garnish with freshly grated Parmesan cheese.

Serves 4.

Roasted Taber Corn, Prosciutto
and Ricotta Ravioli with Creamy Tomato Sauce

Suede Lounge, Edmonton, AB

Taber, Alberta, known as the "Canadian Capital of Corn," has developed its own variety renowned for its sweet, succulent flavour. This recipe from Chef John Setterlund exemplifies its merits, although you can substitute any variety of fresh sweet corn.

2 cups (500 mL) Taber corn kernels
1 tbsp (15 mL) olive oil
1 oz (30 g) prosciutto, diced
¼ cup (60 mL) ricotta cheese
leaves from 2 sprigs fresh thyme
salt and pepper
1lb (500 g) wonton wrappers
1 egg, beaten
Creamy Tomato Sauce (recipe follows)

Preheat oven to 350°F (180°C). Remove kernels from cob into a roasting pan and drizzle with olive oil. Roast until golden brown, about 10 minutes. Cool.

Place prosciutto, ricotta cheese, thyme leaves and corn into a food processor and purée. Season to taste with salt and pepper.

Using a wonton sealer, take one wonton wrapper and place 1 tbsp (15 mL) of corn mixture in the middle. Brush egg lightly around the edges and seal. Repeat procedure until filling has been used and you have about 20 wontons.

Bring a large pot of lightly salted water to a boil. Add wontons a few at a time and cook until they float to the surface, about 7 minutes. Remove from water, drain and keep warm.

To serve: arrange wontons on plates. Top with Creamy Tomato Sauce.

Serves 4.

Creamy Tomato Sauce
1 ½ tsp (7 mL) vegetable oil
½ yellow onion, finely diced
1 large carrot, finely diced
3 stalks celery, finely diced
1 bay leaf
1 tbsp (15 mL) fresh thyme
1 tbsp (15 mL) chopped fresh basil
1 cup (250 mL) white wine
4 large vine-ripened tomatoes, cut into small dice
1 x 14 oz (398 g) can diced tomatoes
2 cloves garlic, minced
salt and pepper
2 tbsp (30 mL) heavy cream (35% m.f.)

Heat oil in a heavy-based saucepan over low heat and sweat onion, carrot, celery and herbs until vegetables are translucent, about 20 minutes. Stir in wine, tomatoes and garlic and simmer on medium heat about 45 minutes. In a food processor, purée in batches and adjust seasoning. Bring to a simmer and stir in heavy cream.

Makes 4 cups.

Rigatoni with Tomato, Basil
and Mushroom Sauce

Hemispheres Restaurant & Bistro, The Metropolitan Hotel, Toronto, ON

The secret to the wonderful earthy flavour of this sauce lies in the variety of mushrooms used. At Hemisphere's Restaurant & Bistro the sauce is served with rigatoni pasta, but all varieties of pasta are suitable.

The chef comments that the sauce may be prepared in advance, covered and refrigerated. Simply rewarm before continuing.

4 tbsp (60 mL) olive oil, portioned
⅓ cup (75 mL) minced shallot
3 garlic cloves, minced and divided
4 oz (125 g) shiitake mushrooms, stemmed, caps thinly sliced
4 oz (125 g) oyster mushrooms, thinly sliced
4 oz (125 g) baby portobello mushrooms, thinly sliced
4 oz (125 g) button mushrooms, thinly sliced
¾ cup (175 mL) chopped onion
1 shallot, thinly sliced
1 x 28 oz (796 mL) can diced Italian tomatoes
½ cup (125 mL) dry white wine
½ cup (125 mL) chopped fresh basil, divided
salt and pepper
12 oz (375 g) rigatoni pasta

¼ cup (60 mL) grated Parmesan cheese
¼ cup (60 mL) drained oil-packed sun-dried tomatoes, thinly sliced
additional grated Parmesan cheese, for serving

Heat half of the olive oil in a large, heavy skillet over medium heat. Add minced shallot and 1 minced garlic clove and sauté until tender, about 5 minutes. Increase heat to medium-high, add all mushrooms and sauté, stirring constantly until tender, about 5 minutes. Transfer mushrooms to a bowl.

Heat remaining olive oil in the same skillet over medium heat. Add onion, sliced shallot and remaining minced garlic; sauté until tender, about 5 minutes. Add diced tomatoes and white wine and simmer 10 minutes. Stir in mushroom mixture and ¼ cup (60 mL) of fresh basil. Remove from heat, adjust seasoning with salt and pepper, cover and keep warm.

Cook pasta in a large pot of boiling salted water until *al dente*, stirring occasionally. Drain well and return pasta to pot. Add mushroom sauce and toss to coat pasta. Add Parmesan cheese and toss to coat.

To serve: transfer to a large warmed serving dish and sprinkle with sun-dried tomatoes and remaining chopped basil. Add additional Parmesan cheese separately, as desired.

Serves 4.

Roma Tomato Sauce with Roasted Garlic,
Sweet Onion and Basil

Keefer Mansion Inn, Thorold, ON

The key to a fabulous sauce is to use only fresh, succulent, vine-ripened tomatoes, so this is the perfect pasta sauce to make when tomatoes are at the height of their harvesting season. You can add meats, seafood or vegetables to this sauce but it stands well on its own without additional ingredients.

Roasted Garlic (recipe follows)
Puréed Fresh Basil (recipe follows)
¼ cup (60 mL) olive oil
1 sweet onion, finely diced (Vidalia, Mayan, Walla Walla, etc.)
3 large shallots, julienned lengthwise
1 tbsp (15 mL) brown sugar
½ cup (125 mL) red wine
3 lb (750 g) vine ripe Roma tomatoes, peeled and chopped
1 tbsp (15 mL) balsamic vinegar
1 tsp (5 mL) freshly ground black pepper
salt
pasta of choice to serve 4 to 6
grated Parmigiano-Reggiano cheese

Prepare roasted garlic and basil purée.

In a heavy-based saucepan or sauté pan heat oil over medium heat. Add onion and shallots and sweat until translucent, about 8 minutes. Add brown sugar and caramelize, stirring frequently, until bottom of pan turns golden, about 12 to 15 minutes.

Add red wine and deglaze pan using a wooden spoon to remove all the pieces from the bottom of the pan; reduce until almost dry. Add tomatoes and roasted garlic and simmer until tomatoes break down, about 10 minutes. Reduce heat to very low and stew 30 to 40 minutes. Depending upon the water content of the tomatoes, you may have to add a little water to avoid burning. Adjust seasoning with puréed basil, balsamic vinegar, pepper and salt to taste. Return to serving temperature.

Prepare pasta until *al dente*, then drain.

To serve: portion pasta into pasta bowls, and top with sauce. Garnish with Parmigiano-Reggiano cheese.

Serves 4 to 6.

Roasted Garlic

1 whole garlic bulb
1 tsp (5 mL) olive oil

Preheat oven to 350°F (180°C). Rub loose skin from garlic bulb. Trim root end flat and snip tip end from each clove; be careful not to detach individual cloves. Set bulb on a sheet of aluminum foil and drizzle oil over it. Enclose bulb with foil and place in oven. Roast until soft, about 1 hour.

Unwrap garlic, cool slightly and squeeze out individual cloves through the cut end. Mash garlic in a small bowl and reserve.

Puréed Fresh Basil

1 bunch fresh basil, about 2 to 3 oz (55 to 85 g)
1 or 2 ice cubes

In a blender, combine basil with ice cubes and blend until puréed. Remove to a small bowl and cover with plastic wrap directly touching purée to keep it from oxidizing; reserve.

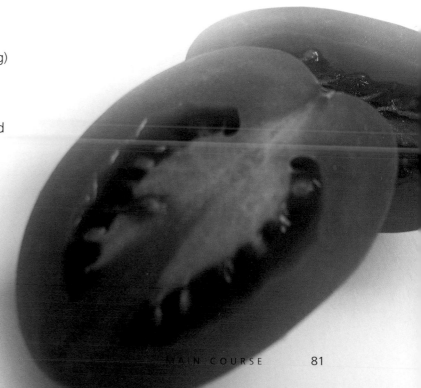

Green Tomato and Apple Chutney, p. 93

Sides and Condiments

To accompany our main course recipes and add a little variety to your daily vegetable requirements we invite you try our selection of side dishes. Easy to prepare Baked Campari Tomatoes will add vibrant colour to your dish and Mahle House Restaurant's Provençal Vegetables is a vegetable meal in itself. In each recipe the chef calls for the freshest veggies available.

In our opinion, home-prepared condiments take a meal from the ordinary to the sublime. We all have fond memories of gathering around the family dinner table on a Sunday evening when grandma would serve her favourite pickle or chow. For that reason we have included Tomato Fruit Relish, a Mennonite recipe handed down from generation to generation in Ontario's Niagara region, where fresh vegetables and fruit are abundant; and Green Tomato Chow Chow, a recipe from our family collection.

Oven Roasted
Plum Tomatoes

The Blomidon Inn, Wolfville, NS

Fresh from the inn's gardens, these succulent slow-roasted tomatoes add punch to pasta dishes, salads or as an accompaniment to wild game and other meats. They are so good you might just want to pop them in your mouth for a quick flavourful snack.

2 tbsp (30 mL) minced garlic
2 tsp (10 mL) chopped fresh thyme
1 tbsp (15 mL) chopped fresh basil
2 tsp (10 mL) chopped fresh oregano
3 tbsp (45 mL) balsamic vinegar
2 tbsp (30 mL) extra virgin olive oil
12 Roma tomatoes, cut in wedges

Preheat oven to 275°F (136°C). In a bowl, whisk together all ingredients except tomatoes until blended. Add tomatoes and toss to coat.

Line a rimmed baking sheet with foil. Arrange tomatoes in a single layer on foil and bake 2 hours, or until tomatoes have lost their moisture.

Makes 1 ½ cups (375 mL).

Provençal
Vegetables

The Mahle House Restaurant, Nanaimo, BC

This colourful side dish makes a delicious accompaniment to almost any main dish, especially grilled seafood and meats.

2 tbsp (30 mL) olive oil, portioned
1 medium onion, diced
2 small zucchini, seeded and diced
1 Japanese eggplant, diced
1 each, red and yellow pepper, cored, seeded and diced
2 cups (500 mL) fresh plum tomatoes, diced
2 tbsp (30 mL) basil pesto (pre-prepared, or use recipe p. 57)

Heat 1 ½ tsp (7 mL) olive oil in a heavy skillet over medium heat and sauté onion, stirring frequently, until softened. Remove to a bowl. Repeat process with peppers, zucchini and eggplant, sautéeing each separately and adding olive oil as needed. When cooked, remove each vegetable to the bowl with the onion.

Return all cooked vegetables to the skillet; add diced tomatoes and pesto and cook briefly to incorporate flavours.

Serves 4.

Tomato Fruit
Relish

Lakewinds Country Manor, Niagara-on-the-Lake, ON

What to do when you have an abundance of autumn's bounty? At Lakewinds Country Manor innkeeper Steve Locke prepares this delicious Mennonite-style relish to serve with quiche, cold meats and his traditional Christmas Eve tourtière.

20 medium-sized ripe tomatoes
8 pears, peeled, cored and cubed
8 peaches, peeled, pitted and cubed
6 onions, finely diced
2 red peppers, seeded, cored and diced
4 cups (1 L) granulated sugar
4 cups (1 L) white vinegar
2 tbsp (20 mL) pickling spices, tied in a
    cheesecloth bag
1 ½ tbsp (22 mL) salt

Place all ingredients in a large, heavy-based saucepan. Cook over high heat until mixture begins to boil. Reduce heat and simmer, stirring frequently until very thick and no liquid remains, about 1 ½ to 2 hours.

Pour into sterilized jars and seal. Process jars in a boiling water bath 10 minutes. Remove, cool jars and store in a cool, dark place.

Makes 10 to 12 x 8 oz (250 mL) jars.

Keltic
Ketchup

Keltic Lodge, Ingonish Beach, NS

Why make ketchup, you might ask? We promise that once you have tasted Executive Chef Dale Nichols' flavourful condiment you will never buy commercial ketchup again!

2 tbsp (30 mL) canola oil
1 medium yellow onion, peeled and finely diced
2 tbsp (30 mL) minced garlic
2 medium-sized ripe tomatoes, cored and diced
1 cup (250 mL) canned tomato sauce
1 cup (250 mL) white vinegar
½ cup (125 mL) water
⅓ cup (75 mL) raisins
½ cup (125 mL) molasses
¼ cup (60 mL) lightly packed brown sugar
1 tbsp (15 mL) ground allspice
14 to 16 dashes Worcestershire sauce
pinch of ground cloves or mace
salt and freshly ground black pepper

Heat oil until hot but not smoking in a heavy-based saucepan over medium heat. Add onion and cook until translucent, stirring occasionally, 5 to 7 minutes. Add garlic and cook, stirring often, 1 minute. Add all remaining ingredients and bring to a boil. Reduce heat to low and simmer, uncovered, stirring occasionally, 1 hour or until slightly thickened.

Remove from heat and purée in batches in a food processor or blender until smooth. Refrigerated in a sealed container, the ketchup will keep 4 to 6 weeks.

Makes 3 cups (750 mL).

Green Tomato
Chow Chow

Oh, what to do with that abundant supply of green tomatoes? You know, the ones that refuse to ripen after the first frost. Use them to make this tasty accompaniment to fall and winter fare.

20 cups (5 L) green tomatoes
6 large onions, thinly sliced
⅓ cup (75 mL) coarse pickling salt
4 cups (1 L) cider vinegar
6 cups (1.5 L) granulated sugar
¼ cup (60 mL) pickling spice (tied in a
    cheesecloth bag)

Wash and thinly slice unpeeled tomatoes, place in a large glass bowl. Thinly slice onions and place in bowl with tomatoes. Sprinkle with pickling salt, stirring to cover vegetables evenly. Cover vegetables and let stand overnight at room temperature.

Thoroughly rinse vegetables with cold running water and press out excess moisture. In a large saucepan bring vinegar and sugar to a boil and add bagged pickling spice. Stir vegetables into vinegar and simmer until liquid has thickened and vegetables are soft, about 1 ½ hours. Ladle into hot sterilized jars and seal. Process jars in boiling water bath 10 minutes. Remove, cool jars and store in a cool dark cupboard up to 1 year.

Makes 12 cups (3 L).

Heirloom Tomato
Salsa

Chives Canadian Bistro, Halifax, NS

Chef Craig Flinn notes that the beauty of this accompaniment is in its colour, texture, and pure tomato flavour — if the tomatoes are perfectly ripe, of course! Field tomatoes are great for this dish as they add a meaty texture without a lot of excess water. Serve this salsa with roast chicken, bruschetta, grilled halibut or as a dip with tortilla chips.

1 large field tomato, diced
1 large yellow vine-ripened tomato, diced
2 green zebra tomatoes, quartered
3 cups mixed cherry and grape tomatoes, halved
2 tbsp (30 mL) minced red onion
2 tbsp (30 mL) chopped fresh basil
3 tbsp (45 mL) chopped chives
2 tbsp (30 mL) balsamic vinegar
¼ cup (60 mL) extra virgin olive oil
3 dashes Tabasco sauce
sea salt

In a large bowl combine tomatoes, onion, basil and chives. In a separate bowl whisk together vinegar, olive oil and Tabasco sauce. Pour over tomatoes and toss to coat. Adjust seasoning with sea salt. Set aside at room temperature 1 hour, then serve.

Makes 6 cups (1.5 L).

Tapenade

The Mahle House Restaurant, Nanaimo, BC

Mediterranean flavours abound in this easy-to-prepare condiment. Serve it with crackers, breads and cheese. It is also a good accompaniment to chicken and fish dishes.

½ cup (125 mL) sun-dried tomatoes
1 cup (250 mL) pitted kalamata olives
1 cup (250 mL) manzanilla olives with pimento
2 garlic cloves
1 tbsp (15 mL) drained capers (optional anchovy fillets)
1 tsp (5 mL) chipotle pepper
2 tsp (10 mL) balsamic vinegar
2 to 3 tbsp (30 to 45 mL) extra virgin olive oil
salt and pepper

In a food processor, combine all ingredients except olive oil and salt and pepper; pulse, scraping mixture down sides of the processor until finely chopped. With motor running, add enough olive oil in a steady stream until mixture forms a paste. Adjust seasoning with salt and pepper. (If olives or anchovies are salty you may not need additional salt.)

Store in a jar, refrigerated, up to 2 weeks. Bring to room temperature before serving.

Makes 2 cups (500 mL).

Stuffed Heirloom
Tomatoes

Chanterelle Country Inn, North River, NS

Here is a dish that relies upon the freshness of its ingredients, especially organically grown tomatoes, notes chef and owner Earlene Bush. At the inn she serves the tomatoes with seafood or poultry.

1 large red bell pepper, roasted*
1 cup (250 mL) fresh breadcrumbs
1 garlic clove, minced
pinch cayenne pepper
dash of salt
2 to 3 tbsp (30 to 45 mL) extra virgin olive oil
2 tbsp (30 mL) flax or sesame seeds, lightly
   toasted**
4 medium-sized heirloom tomatoes, cut in half,
   seeded and pulp removed

In a food processor, pulse roasted pepper, breadcrumbs, garlic, cayenne pepper and salt. Slowly pour olive oil through the feeding tube and pulse until mixture binds; adjust seasoning.

Spoon mixture into tomato halves and sprinkle with toasted seeds. Serve chilled.

Serves 4.

* To roast a red pepper: preheat oven to 400°F (200°C). On a baking sheet, roast red pepper whole, turning 2 to 3 times until skin is charred, about 20 minutes. Remove from oven and place pepper in plastic or paper bag, seal and set aside until cool enough to handle. Slide charred skin from pepper; core and remove seeds and membrane.

** To toast flax or sesame seeds: sprinkle seeds in a heavy nonstick frying pan and stir over low heat until lightly toasted.

Quick-Baked Campari
Tomatoes

Sweet little Campari tomatoes, a gift to North America from Europe, are easy to prepare and provide brilliant colour to your entrée. Depending upon their size, allow 2 to 3 per serving.

8 to 12 Campari tomatoes, stems intact
extra virgin olive oil
freshly ground sea salt

Preheat oven to 375° F (190°C). Arrange tomatoes in a baking dish. Drizzle tops with a small amount of olive oil and lightly sprinkle with sea salt. Bake in oven until heated through and skins begin to wrinkle, about 10 to 12 minutes, depending on size.

Serves 4.

Green Tomato
and Apple Chutney

Inn on the Cove & Spa, Saint John, NB

Owners Ross and Willa Mavis comment that this chutney is great with curry. They add that it is wonderful served with pork, turkey and beef dishes. Its spicy yet subtle fruitiness is a perfect complement to the rich flavour of many meat entrées. This recipe was originally featured in the Mavis' cookbook, *Tide's Table* (Goose Lane Editions, 1996).

3 cups (750 mL) diced green tomatoes
2 cups (500 mL) peeled and diced green apples
1 ½ cups (375 mL) raisins
1 cup (250 mL) minced onion
1 garlic clove, minced
1 ½ tsp (7 mL) salt
1 tbsp (15 mL) lemon zest
1 tbsp (15 mL) lemon juice
2 cups (500 mL) white vinegar
¼ tsp (1 mL) cayenne pepper
1 tbsp (15 mL) ground allspice
1 tbsp (15 mL) ground cloves
2 tbsp (30 mL) mustard seeds
2 ½ cups (650 mL) brown sugar
2 tbsp (30 mL) peeled and minced fresh
  gingerroot (tied in a cheesecloth bag)

Combine all ingredients in a large, heavy saucepan and bring to a boil. Reduce heat and simmer, partially covered until thick, about 2 hours. Remove gingerroot.

Pour into sterilized jars and seal. Process jars in a boiling water bath 10 minutes. Remove, cool jars and store in a cool, dark place.

Makes 6 to 8 x 8 oz (250 mL) jars.

Index

Library and Archives Canada Cataloguing in Publication

Elliot, Elaine, 1939-
    Tomatoes : recipes from Canada's best chefs / Elaine Elliot and Virginia Lee.

(Flavours series)
Includes index.
ISBN 978-0-88780-728-2

    1. Cookery (Tomatoes). I. Lee, Virginia, 1947- II. Title. III. Series.

TX803.T6E45 2007   641.6'5642   C2007-903105-6

Photo Credits

All photos by Alanna Jankov with the exception of the following:
Agis Agisilaou: 8 (centre); Trevor Allen: 67; Hamid Attie: 31; Melissa Carroll: 86;
Meghan Collins: 1, 9 (top), 2, 24, 47, 63, 81; Dwayne Coon: 92; Jim Jurica: 6; Travis
Manley: 7, 43; Catherine Oakeson: 84; Dragasanu Mihai Octavian: 9 (centre); Gary
Ogle, Vesey's Seeds Ltd.: 9 (centre); Angus Plummer: 8 (centre); Clint Sholz: 8
(bottom); Suzannah Skelton: 3, 8; Emily Tregunno: 9 (bottom).